Bedtime Stories & Guided Meditations For Busy Adults (2 in 1): Beginners Meditation & Stories For Overcoming Insomnia, Stress Relief, Anxiety, Relaxation & Deep Sleep Hypnosis

By Meditation Made Effortless

Bedtime Stories & Guided Meditations for Busy Adults:

Beginner Meditation & Relaxing Deep Sleep Stories For Insomnia, Stress-Relief, Anxiety, Mindfulness & A Full Nights Rest

Contents

Anxiety Guided Meditation (30mns) 1

Stress Relieving Guided Meditation (30mns) 6

Guided Meditation to Reduce Anxiety (30mns) 10

Morning Anxiety Reducing Meditation to Kick Start Your Day! (30mns) 15

Guided Mindfulness Meditation to Help Reduce Stress and Anxiety (20mns) 19

After Work Stress Relieving Meditation (30mns) 22

Before Sleep Deep Relaxation Meditation (30mns) 27

Guided Meditation for Deep Sleep (30mns) 31

Panic Attack Relaxation meditation (10mns) 34

Morning Mood Booster Meditation (10mns) 36

Lunchtime Relaxation Meditation (15mns) 38

Quick Anxiety Reducing Meditation (15mns) 40

Guided Self-Healing Meditation (30mns) 42

Easy to Follow Self-Healing Meditation (20mns) 46

Guided Sleep Meditation (20mns) 49

Stress Relief Meditation (30mns) 52

Calming After a Panic Attack Meditation (20mns) 57

Deep Relaxation Meditation (20mns) 59

Adult Bedtime Story 1 (60mns) 62

Sleep Hypnosis for Deep Sleep and Relaxation (60mns) 71

Before Sleep Hypnosis for Relaxation (60mns) 76

Anxiety Guided Meditation (30mns)

Hello and welcome to this anxiety-relieving guided meditation. In today's session, we will go on a journey toward inner peace. At the end of this journey, your consciousness will return to reality and your body, mind, and soul will be replenished and rejuvenated.

Without further, go ahead and get into a comfortable position, be it laying down or sitting up. Comfort is of the utmost importance when you need to attain full relaxation.

Right now, you do not even have to close your eyes. Just take a deep breath now and relax. Tell your body and mind that now is the time to unwind and relax. There is nothing else you need to do right now but to enjoy the stillness of the present moment.

Right now, you just have to breathe. Your eyes and mind may wander, but that is quite alright. Let them wander as they please. Sometimes, the key to calming the mind is to let it run and expend all energy. After that, you can bring it under your control.

Take another deep breath and feel your mind becoming stiller and calmer. At each breath you take, you are bringing more relaxation.

Through your nose, inhale slowly and let the air fill your lungs. Hold your breath at the top for 3 seconds. Then, through your mouth, exhale slowly. Feel the air flowing through your body through the entire breathing cycle.

Excellent. Now, continue to do this for a minute.

(Pause 1mn)

Perfect. Now, as you breathe in, slowly close your eyes. With your eyes closed, feel the stillness in your body as you hold your breath for that 3 seconds. After that, open your eyes again as you exhale. Again, feel how the air flows in and out of your body. This time, you just have to open and close your eyes as you inhale and exhale. This time, you just have to notice the stillness when you hold your breath. We will work toward bringing this stillness to calm the mind and relax the body. Continue to do this for another minute.

(Pause 1mn)

Right now, your eyes should feel very heavy and you might want to close your eyes. If so, go ahead and close your eyes now. Now is the time to dive deeply into relaxation. Now is the time to work on relaxing the mind and body.

As your vision fades to black, shift your focus to your breathing. Continue to breathe just like you have been and focus intensely on the sensations you feel as you breathe. Continue to do this for another minute.

(Pause 1mn)

Excellent. You may now continue to breathe as you normally would. At this point, your mind might still wander from one thought to another. It might bring up some random memory. Some of it might be a pleasant memory back from your childhood when things were simple. Some thoughts might be disturbing. The mind may bring up embarrassing secrets about yourself. It might bring up the very thought that caused your anxiety in the first place.

We have given the mind enough time to roam as it pleased. Now, we bring it under control. Throughout this session, whenever your mind wanders, simply guide it back to your breathing.

As we go along, sinking deeper and deeper into relaxation, continue to breathe deeply. Feel the air completely filling your lungs. Breathe deeply and as you do so, feel your body soaking up all that positive energy. When you exhale, feel the negative energy being swept away by the power of your breath alone.

Now, let us work on relaxing the body. You see, whenever the mind thinks of distressing thoughts, the body becomes nervous and twitchy. You cannot function at your best like this.

Therefore, by soothing the body, one also soothes the mind that is the center of anxiety. We can achieve this through the power of breathing alone. But first, let us start with a simple body scan exercise and then use the healing power of breathing to soothe any areas that are tense or stressed.

First, bring your attention to your toes. Wiggle your toes and feel where they are tense or sore. If you notice any tension in your toes, let it melt away as you breathe.

Now bring your attention to your feet. Wiggle your feet a little bit. Tense and flex the muscles in your feet as tightly as you can and then let it go. Feel the tension in your feet melt away and allow them to relax.

What about your ankles? Shift your attention to that area now. Perhaps move your feet around a little bit to engage your ankles. Allow them to relax as much as possible. Scan your ankles for any points of tension and just let it all melt away as you breathe.

Now focus on your calf muscles on the bottom half of your legs. Squeeze your calf muscles tightly and then let go. Relax completely and let all the tension in your legs melt away.

Next focus on your knees. Is there any soreness or tension in your knees? Where are they sore? Now, tense your body as tightly as you possibly can and hold, before completely releasing and relaxing your whole body.

Clenched every muscle tightly…
And relax, letting go…
And again, tense your body as tightly as you can.
Tighten your body as if you are squeezing out all the tension from your body…
And relax, letting go now of all the tension and completely relaxing your body…
For the final time, tense your body as tightly as you can…
Squeeze every muscle as hard as you can…
And relax… letting go now of all the tension and completely, relaxing your body.

Now, go through your body again and focus on each and every area of your body. Look for any tense or stressed areas. If you ever find one, imagine that the breath you take in flows directly to that area and wash away all the stress or tension.

Your body knows what it needs to unwind and relax. You just need to continue to breathe and introduce that healing energy into your body through your nose and push away all the negative energy as you exhale.

Let your knees complete relax… Unwind and relax…

Now focus on the upper half of your legs. Without moving your legs too much, tense up your upper leg muscles and then relax them and let go. Feel the tension you keep in your legs melt away and become fully relaxed.

Now bring your attention to your pelvic area. Feel where your body is sitting or lying. Feel where your pelvis touches the seat or where it touches where you are lying. Scan for areas of tension or discomfort.

Now, imagine that the air that you breathe in has a bright yellow color to it, imagine that it has powerful healing energy and that your body is soaking up all of its positive energy to heal as you breathe.

Introduce that energy to every part of your body and feel as your muscles relax and your tension starts to drift away. Now bring your attention to your lower back. Many of us carry around tension in our lower backs. Where do you feel pain?

Visualize yourself sending healing energy to these areas and feel the tension being to melt away. Next move your attention to the font of your body, your stomach. Feel your stomach rise and fall as you breathe in and out.

Our stomachs are often where we feel things first, this is why we say things like "I have a gut feeling this is a good or bad idea. It's also why we often get indigestion or nausea when we are dealing with highly stressful events.

Allow your stomach to lengthen, to soften, to relax. Feel all the tension in your stomach melt away as you breathe. Now, continue to bring this positive energy with your breathing up to your chest, your heart, the center of your being.

Maybe you can feel or hear your heart beating. Allow yourself to fully experience this. Allow all tension in the body to fade away as you exhale. Next, bring your attention to your upper back behind your chest.

Our upper back suffers a lot from both the stress we carry and our long hours sitting at work, often typing on computers. Feel your breath enter your body and your ribs expand. Breath out all of the tension and stress in your back and completely relax.

Next, shift your focus to your shoulders, which is another common place for tension. Perhaps you sometimes feel like you are carrying the weight of the world on your shoulders alone. Perhaps you do not have to carry this burden alone. Even if you do, now is not the time to carry it. Now is the time to unwind and relax…

And so, introduce that healing aura to your shoulders and let them droop down, let them rest in their natural position. Feel all the stress and tension released, as it slowly drifts away.

What about your neck? Does it feel sore or tense? If so, where? Where are you holding onto tension? As you exhale, allow the air to wash away all that tension and stress from your neck. Feel it becoming softer and softer, no longer rigid as you normally feel.

Now, let us focus on your face. Allow your mouth, cheek, jaw, and tongue to relax, to loosen, and to return to their natural positions. Squint up your face as hard as you can and then let it all go. Relax your face muscles and let the tension melt away.

Move your focus to your eyes and forehead. Are you squeezing your eyes? Are you furrowing your brows? Is your forehead relaxed? Are you holding tension here? If so, continue to breathe intently and feel the soothing aura going to that area and relaxes it. Feel this tension melt away as you begin to fully relax.

Lastly, bring your attention to the top and back of your head. Is there any tension here? If so, allow your breath to carry away all that tension. Continue to breathe intently and allow your breathing to carry away all the tension and stress from your body.

By now you should be fully relaxed. Enjoy this feeling. When you are ready, simply take a deep breath and slowly open your eyes. This concludes our meditation. Thank you and have a nice day.

Stress Relieving Guided Meditation (30mns)

Hello and welcome to this stress relieving guided meditation. In this session, we will work toward unwinding and relaxing the mind and body after a long day of work. Without further ado, let's get started.

Start by getting into a comfortable position. You can either sit or lay down, whatever works for you. It is fine so long as you are comfortable. After all, comfort is very important for a productive meditation session.

Once you are ready, go ahead and close your eyes. Take a few deep breaths now to tell your body that it is time to relax. On your next breath in, inhale through your nose, holding your breath at the top and count to 3 before exhaling through your mouth.

Slowly breathing in… 1… 2… 3… And slowly out…

Excellent. Now continue to do this for a while.

(Pause 1mn)

At this point, your mind may start to wander. It might bring up certain thoughts, some are positive and others are negative. Whatever those thoughts are, simply acknowledge their existence and shift your focus back to your breathing. But do not beat yourself up for it because it is natural for the mind to wander from time to time.

Now, you may allow your breathing to return to its natural rhythm. Let us work on washing away the stress in your body. So as you breathe, scan through your body and notice any tension in your body.

Starting from the top of your head, slowly shift your focus down your body. Focus on the forehead now and notice whether your forehead is tense. If it is, allow your breathing to soothe that area. Feel the air flowing in to your forehead and feel it brushing gently against your forehead as if it is gently brushing away the tension in your forehead.

Repeat this process as you go down, to the brows, eyelids, nose, cheek, jaw, lips… If you are holding onto any tension in any of those areas, use the power of your breathing to brush away the tension.

Allow your jaw to slack slightly and your tongue to return to their natural position. Take another deep breath again and feel every muscle in your head relaxing just as you exhale.

Going down to the torso now… Allow your shoulders to rest and your chest to expand and contract gently as you breathe. Feel your stomach rising and falling as you continue to breathe deeply, filling your lungs with the air that your body needs to relax. Feel your back relaxing at each breath.

Send down that positive and relaxing energy to your arms and legs. Feel the muscles in that area becoming soft and relaxed. Allow your fingers to return to their natural positions.

As you breathe, scan through your body again and notice any tense muscles in your body…

Let your breathing soothes those muscles… As if the air you let out takes away the tension in your body…

You may notice that your face is tense, or you may notice certain areas of your body are tense that you did not realize before…

You can only see them once you are in deep relaxation…

So, breathe…

In…

And out…

Let's start with thoroughly relaxing your entire body, just with deep breathing. Start intentionally breathing deep and slow now…

(Pause 2mn)

Try not to hold any parts of your body in any position… Relax and let them fall into their natural resting position…

Now, picture yourself at the beach on a beautiful sunny day. The sky above is deep blue and you could see some white clouds drifting slowly. You notice one that looks like a rabbit. The other, a face. They drift across the sky in an unhurried pace as the gentle breeze blows by.

Take a deep breath now and feel this warm breeze brushing against your body and feel yourself sinking deeper into relaxation. Focus on the warmth of the sun and use that warmth to help you to begin to help you begin to relax all of the muscles of your body.

Feel every part of your body becoming enveloped by this pleasant and relaxing sensation, from the top of your head down to your toes. Your entire body is now drenched in the warmth of the sun. Feel your every nerve and muscle becoming heavy and relaxed.

Your breathing is deep, slow, and easy. You are calm. You are at peace as you drift deeper and deeper into a state of relaxation and peace.

Take another deep breath now and feel the warm breeze washing over you. Smell that saltiness in the air. You can hear seagulls in the distance. It is indeed a wonderfully warm and peaceful day.

You look down now and see the white sand below your feet.

As you wiggle your toes to feel the fine, ivory sand slinking between your toes, you notice a few small, vibrant shells close by.

Feel yourself becoming more and more relaxed as you appreciate this feeling and quiet moment You listen to the sound of the wave washing over the shore, crashing over the breach, and flow back out again.

Synchronize your breathing with the waves. As they crash in, breathe in. As they flow back out to the sea, exhale. With each wave, you can feel yourself becoming more and more relaxed… More and more comfortable… And more and more at peace…

Any discomforts you may be feeling now start to dissipate with each wave. As you look out over the surface of the ocean, the water is crystal clear and you can see the sands swirling softly beneath the water as each wave come and go.

Look over the horizon and notice sailboats in the distance as they glide along the surface of the water. You watch the cloud move and change shape above you.

Notice the seagulls gliding over the sea. Imagine yourself riding on their backs and going far beyond the vast expanse of the sea.

Now, take in a deep breath.
Breathe in…
And out…

Feel yourself becoming warmer, cozier, more relaxed, and comfortable. Feel the sun overhead and appreciate the sense of warmth that starts from the top of your head and flowing down to your toes, allowing you to relax completely.

You now lay down a blanket on the beach and lie down to sunbathe. You feel the warmth of the sun washing over your entire body. You close your eyes and settle in, feeling relaxed even more.

It is a lovely day. You just lay there and listen to the soothing sound of the crashing waves. Each wave washes away your tensions and worries, carrying them away out to the sea.

You are now fully settled into your sanctuary. You can return to this place whenever you wish to find a sense of deep relaxation and comfort.

You may notice a symbol or shape that represents this place. Think of the symbol as the key to enter this wonderful, comfortable safe haven.

Thinking of this symbol alone helps you relax. You can access this place at any time as it is available to you at all times.

Now, it is time to return to the real world once more. Whenever you are ready, count down from 5 to 1.

As you count, you become more and more alert until you become fully awake at one, while still maintaining this deep sense of peace and relaxation. Let us begin…

5… Slowly coming back now…

4…

3… Starting to coming back to reality…

2… You can now open your eyes.

1… You are fully relaxed. Thank you and have a nice day.

Guided Meditation to Reduce Anxiety (30mns)

Hello and welcome to this guided anxiety reduction meditation. In this session, we will help you give your body that much-needed break from all your anxiety, a liberation from tension, and to give you a state of physical and mental calmness by focusing on breathing, observing the state of your body, relaxing your tense muscles, and to calm your thoughts.

So let us begin. Get into a comfortable position and lay down in your bed. You may put your arms and legs however you want as long as you are comfortable. If at any point during this session, you start to feel any discomfort, you can move your body a bit to ease that discomfort.

Go ahead and inhale slowly and deeply as your eyes close. As your vision fades to black, take another deep breath and notice how the air flows in and out of your body. Take a third deep breath and signal to the body and mind that it is time to unwind and relax.

Keep this slow and steady breathing, completely filling and emptying your lungs at each breath. Your deep breathing relaxes and calms you. It allows your body to relax, to get enough oxygen, and to feel calm.

Remain in this position. There is nothing you need to do right now and nowhere you need to be. You just need to be here, relax, and enjoy this time for yourself.

Take your time and enjoy this time for yourself. Maybe you have been through a lot, you know? Your body and mind are tired and yet you might feel that you could do something much more. Maybe you are worried about a future event. Maybe you are worried that you are not good enough.

But whatever you might be thinking right now, you do not have to worry about it now. This is the time to unwind and relax. This relaxation time will help you to be calm and healthy. This session is your productive, health time. You are doing yourself a favor by taking care of your mental health with this sleep anxiety relaxation meditation.

As you maintain your deep and steady breathing, turn your attention to your body. Notice how it feels physically. Do not do anything about it. Just be aware of the sensations in your body.

At this point, you just have to observe your body and let it tell you where the tensions are. The mind and body will guide you. Whatever it is you feel right now, recognize that it is okay. You should not concern with your physical sensations. However, some pleasant ones may be because they are signs of built-up stress.

So, take a moment and notice how you are feeling. Note any signs of stress and tension you have, again, without trying to do anything about it yet.

Scan your entire body, from the top of your head and move downward slowly.

Start focusing on your head. Observe how your head feels against the pillow or whatever beneath it.

Then, start to move your attention down to your eyes, nose, chin, then your shoulders. Notice each area as you focus your attention on it. Observe how your body feels.

Keep scanning your body. Gradually focus your attention on lower and lower parts of your body. How does your upper body feel? Note any areas of tension.

As you move to the center of your body, around the level of your stomach, note how this part of your body is feeling. Keep observing your physical state. Continue to scan your body as you shift your focus lower and lower.

Keep doing this to the level of your hips. Keep observing and shifting your attention down. How do you feel at this part of your body? Notice tensions in this part without trying to change anything. Once again, move your focus downward.

At the level of your knees, again, notice how this area feels. Notice any tension in that area. Continue to look for any signs of tension until you reach your feet.

Now, take another moment to scan your entire body. Note how your body feels as a whole. We will start now and work on soothing that tension in your body.

Starting with the area that causes you the most discomfort, focus intently on that area. On your next breath in, feel that cool breeze going straight to that area, soothing the muscles there. Feel your muscles in that spot loosening up letting go of their tension. Imagine them relaxing, releasing the tension bit by bit until the area relax.

Feel that tension loosening its grip from your body. Feel the muscles loosening up slowly, bit by bit, stretching, relaxing, becoming soft as if they are melting. Continue to do this for the rest of your body until all areas of tension are taken care of.

(Pause 2mns)

Now, on your next breath in, breathe in through your nose, holding it at the top and count to 3, and breathe out. When you hold your breath, notice how it feels. Notice the stillness in the air as you hold your breath. Study its essence as we will introduce its peacefulness to the rest of the body. Continue to breathe this way for another minute.

(Pause 1mn)

Now that you have understood the essence of that tranquil stillness, let us work on introducing this to the body so that you may be thoroughly relaxed. Imagine this sensation spreading from your mind, moving slowly to other parts of the body. Think of it as an aura that flows slowly through your body.

Feel your body becoming more and more relaxed as this stillness, this peacefulness, this magical aura spreads throughout your body. At each breath you take, feel yourself sinking deeper and deeper into relaxation.

Imagine that the air you breathe contains some healing properties, the positive energy that your body needs to relax. Imagine that the air you breathe in is relaxation and peace. As you breathe in, feel your body soaking up all this positive energy. As you breathe out, feel yourself pushing out the tension from your body, just like how the waves recede.

Feel this relaxation as you take each and every breath. Expel the tension in your body as you exhale through your mouth. Continue to take in relaxation through the nose and push out tension through your mouth. Continue doing this as you let your body relax.

Feel yourself becoming more and more relaxed as you continue to breathe.

Breathe in…
And breathe out…
Each breath you take adds to the relaxation. Each breath you push out takes away the tension.
Keep your breathing slow and steady and feel your body becoming more relaxed with each breath. Continue to do this for a minute.

(Pause 1mn)

You now feel calm, relaxed. Your body is calm and your mind is clear… Breathing in relaxation and breathing out relaxation.

Take a deep breath in… and relax…
Now, breathe out… Relax…

Keep your breathing slow and steady. Maintain your pace and feel your body relaxing more and more deeply with each breath you take. You do not need anything now. Just rest and enjoy this relaxing sensation.

(Pause 1mn)

Now, focus on your thoughts. Notice your calm thoughts as you are enjoying this relaxation. You can attain complete calm and relaxation just by focusing on a single word. Meditate now and focus on the word "relax" by mentally saying it each time you breathe in and out.

Breathe in, "relax"
Breathe out, "relax"

Continue your slow and steady breathing, saying "relax" in your mind each time you breathe in and again when you breathe out. Continue doing this for a while.

(Pause 1mn)

It is fine if your mind starts to wander since they will, as it is only natural. Do not beat yourself up for it. Simply guide your focus back to your breathing, and tell yourself to relax. Repeat the word "relax" as you continue with this meditation.

Focus… Relax…
Keep repeating this word…

Notice how you are now completely relaxed and calm, drifting into a state of relaxation and sleepiness. You can let your mind drift. Now is the time to let your mind wander. You do not need to focus on anything at all.

Just… Rest… Relax… And enjoy this pleasant state you are in. Continue to relax and enjoy this pleasant, calm sensation. Enjoy this time you have for yourself. You deserve this peacefulness.

Remember that you have now created a space for yourself. You can return to this place of peace whenever you need to take a break. Even after you leave this place, the feeling of calm will remain with you wherever you go…

This feeling of calm and confidence will be there by your side as you about your daily life, even when you encounter stress… In fact, you can access this place of peace just by thinking about it when you start to feel anxious. You may find that the anxiety goes away in an instant.,

You may even be able to keep this relaxed feeling with you even when you encounter stressful situations. Imagine the confidence and composure you will display as you face stress while still feeling calm.

Take a deep breath in…
Relaxation breathing…
And breathe out… Emptying your lungs…

Keep breathing calmly and smoothly. Maintain this breathing cycle. Taking in relaxation and pushing out the tension that accumulates throughout the day. Imagine how every breath you take helps you become resilient against the harsh reality of life. That you are now able to cope with the stresses that come your way.

As we come to the conclusion of this meditation, you can remain here for as long as you like and enjoy this beautiful beach you have created for yourself. Whenever you are ready to return to reality, simply take a deep breath and slowly open your eyes.

Thank you.

Morning Anxiety Reducing Meditation to Kick Start Your Day! (30mns)

Hello and welcome to this morning anxiety reduction meditation. In this session, we will work on focusing your senses and calming your nerves for whatever it is that awaits you in the near future. Maybe you are anxious about an upcoming interview. Maybe it is a date, perhaps. Whatever the occasion may be, you will feel calm after this session.

So go ahead now and get into a comfortable position. You can sit or lay down however you want so long as you are comfortable. The idea is to thoroughly relax your entire body. Then, close your eyes and shift your focus to your breathing.

Now, start to scan your entire body and noting any tension in your body as well as noticing where you feel a lightness or ease. Then, scan your emotional body to notice any feelings or stress as well as emotional lightness, or something you feel good about….

Then, check in with your mind. Notice if today is one of those days full of worrying thoughts. Or if today is a good day and that you feel peaceful and quiet.

Then, focus on your breathing. Notice how it flows in and out of your body. Feel the air as it fills and deflates your lungs. Notice how your chest gently rises and falls at each breath you take.

You may notice that the air does not flow as smoothly. Maybe your breaths are shallow. Maybe you feel constrained. You can start to take deeper breaths… First into the belly… In… And out…

Then from the chest… In… And out…

Then focus on your upper back as you breathe… In… And out…

Now, repeat the breathing cycle again but holding the breath, starting from the belly… In… Hold… And out…

From the chest… In… Hold… And out…

Focusing on your upper back now… In… Hold… And out…

Breathe deep and slow…

As you continue to breathe, imagine the tension in your body fading away, washed out from your body as you exhale. As you continue to breathe deeply and calmly, check in with your body again and look for any signs of tension.

Let your breathing soothes those nervous, anxious muscles. As if the air you let out takes away the tension in your body. You may notice that your face is tense, or you may notice certain areas of your body are tense that you did not realize before.

You can only see them once you are in deep relaxation…

So, breathe…

In…

And out…

Imagine the breath swirling throughout your body, and sweeping up all the tension in your body and mind before flowing out of your body once more. At each breathe you take, feel it going to every nook and cranny of your body… Your arms, legs, fingertips and toes, ribs and hips, up to the neck, head, and even ears…

At each breath you take, feel your body being nourished and the oxygen going to every place in your body…

At each breath, you take in nourishment your body needs, and let out any stress and tension in your body and mind…

Continue to breathe as you start to clear your mind from any mental chatter, allowing it to be fully focused on sensing the entire body.

Imagine you inhaling clarity, a sense of well-being, and calm, and let them manifest in your body as you hold your breath at the top, and then release stress…

At each breath you take in, you fortify, strengthen, and refresh the body. At each exhale, you let go of all that no longer serves you…

Breathe slowly and deeply…

In…

Hold…

And out…

You choose a memory of how it really feels when you achieve something because many years ago, you achieved many goals. You realized your level of talent because you overcame something big that put you on the path to where you are now and you know that it took courage.

It took perseverance. It took persistence and it took your tenacity to never give up and you never gave up. You did it.

I'm talking about learning to walk. You know at first it wasn't easy pulling yourself up and then sometimes falling down, pulling up, and falling down again. But you persevered. You found the courage from somewhere. There was no way you were giving up and then one day your legs seemed so much stronger.

So much more able to carry your weight. Your whole frame was more stable, more robust because you trusted in yourself as you have really trusted yourself before. And now today, you know you can just put one foot in front of the other without even thinking about it.

At that time there was a massive sense of achievement.

You did this against all odds and as the days and weeks and months go by, you get stronger, faster, and more confident. You never look back and you chose not to look back when you decided to move forward.

When you think in this way and when you feel in this way, you really do know that anything is possible. Anything is possible for you as you contemplate what is ahead.

You can imagine your mind is successful in its stillness and calmness. Just silently enjoying and witnessing these moments of success, fascinated and excited by those abilities that you have deep inside to learn and do whatever it is you need to learn and do.

Your mind knows exactly how to learn and achieve and succeed. It is still with you today. That part of you is still with you right now.

All of those talents that have been hiding within you can now be released and expressed as you become your most authentic, successful, invigorated, and inspired self.

But you can learn new ways of thinking, new ways of responding, new ways of feeling, new ways of acting because the patterns of living that we all do are just patterns.

They really are just a habit that you choose because your mind is so much more powerful and perhaps you even know your mind is so much more powerful than you know.

And just like learning to walk, you can overcome any challenge.

You can overcome any challenge, any barrier, any limiting belief. You can overcome and move past any barrier, any limiting belief as you make the decision now to just let go of those old ways that had previously held you back.

Let go of the old way, soaking up that which is valuable, taking one step at a time.

Slowly, easily, naturally, you are successful. You are inspired. You are motivated.

You know you can do, what you set out to achieve, and now in your own time, allow yourself to become more aware.

Moving up towards the surface now, coming back to the present, and now slowly in your own time. Allow yourself to become more aware or aware of your conscious surroundings. Perhaps gently moving your fingers and your toes.

Becoming aware of your physical sensations and your physical body and when you are ready, gently allow your eyes to open. Moving up now towards the surface of your conscious awareness, coming back fully to the present, feeling refreshed, energized, and motivated to start your new day.

Feeling, refreshed, energized, inspired, and motivated completely to start your very new day. You are now ready to tackle everything in your path. You are unstoppable.

Take your time to enjoy this unhurried moment. Allow yourself to immerse in the meditation and give your body and mind full attention…

Notice any tense areas in your body or mind and breathe away to relax them…

As you come to the end of this meditation session, take another deep breath and smile as you have given yourself time and attention. Slowly open your eyes when you are ready to start your day. Have a great day and I wish you all the very best.

Guided Mindfulness Meditation to Help Reduce Stress and Anxiety (20mns)

Hello and welcome to this guided mindfulness meditation to reduce stress and anxiety. In this session, we will work on relaxing the body and mind, thus liberating them from the grips of stress and anxiety.

To begin, get into a comfortable position. You can either lay down or sit. If at any point during this session, you start to feel any discomfort in any area of your body, you may shift your body a bit to ease that pain.

Without further ago, go ahead and close your eyes now and take a deep breath to tell it that it is time to unwind and relax. Then, let your mind become quiet. Turn your attention inward as you focus on relaxing your body. Let your muscles relax. From the top of your head all the way to the tips of your toes.

Now, think of what relaxation feels like. To you, it might be warm, tingly, maybe heavy yet comfortable, or light and liberating. Whatever it is, relaxation is indeed a calm, pleasant feeling. It is very comfortable.

Allow your muscles to relax and try and find any areas of your body that are tense. We shall start by relaxing the body from there. As your chest rose and fall gently as you breathe, picture yourself breathing in the relaxation in the air every time. As you breathe out, feel the tension and stress leaving your body.

As you breathe out, imagine all the tension leaves your body, riding on the air you let out of your chest. And you become even more relaxed as you breathe in the cool air. Becoming so deeply relaxed. Notice how relaxed you are.

As you breathe, any remaining tension continues to leave your body… And you become more and more relaxed.

Now is the time to relax. You just need to relax. You do not need to do anything else right now but to unwind and relax. Let go of all your worldly worries. Right now, just loosen up and relax.

Now, let's use visualization to focus your mind. Give it a mental break from all the worldly worries. Whenever worrying thoughts intrude your peace of mind, as they will, recall this serene feeling you have in your body at this very moment.

Whenever your peace of mind is intruded by worldly worries, tell yourself to breathe. The rise and fall of your chest will soothe you. Let yourself relax. Then, imagine that worry is a deep and dark place…

And peace you crave for is the light…

Stress and anxiety demand that you stay awake and shaky because of them. It is an evil power and you feel its influence when your muscles start to tense up, even when you are sleeping. It causes sore and ruins your mood, your peace of mind. This is what they do to the mind and body. They make you feel restless and tired.

Think of your peace of mind as light and sleepy element. Think of it as a loving mother, calling to you to come to her embrace. She will tell you to come to her and that she will bring you to a warm and cozy place. She will give you a nice, warm, and soft bed for you to lie on. She will tell you all the things you need to hear for your exhausted mine. She will make you feel safe, at ease. She will take you to a place of tranquility.

Now, using the power of your imagination, think of a place where you would feel peaceful. You do not have to try hard here as your subconscious mind will often take the lead and conjure up such a place.

It could be a place beyond your wildest dreams, a magnificent waterfall, a vast field of vibrant flowers, a mountaintop that pierces the clouds, a golden beach, or a thick and peaceful forest. It could be a place you have been to. Use the power of your imagination to access that place of peace.

You are there now, in the place of peace, where nothing in the world can harm you. This is the place of your own creation. You have been here a few times in the past when you are asleep. Your mind often comes here when you are unconscious.

It comes here to relax and rejuvenate. But it cannot come here often as this place is often locked. To access this place, you need to relax the mind and body. Once you do, the door opens for you. Now that you are here, you can take this place with you to the outside world, along with its powerful yet relaxing aura.

Whenever you feel stressed or anxious, you just have to close your eyes and breathe deeply. You will be transported back to this place and you will feel at ease once more. By then, nothing can harm you.

Now, take a moment to explore this place of your own making. Feel this place with all your senses. Absorb the essence of this place and feel yourself sinking deeper and deeper into relaxation.

Now, repeat this mantra after me.

"Right now, I am at peace. I am surrounded by peace. I am not in danger. Nothing can harm me."

"I am at peace. I can picture happy images with my imagination. I can recall peaceful words I have read or heard today to calm me down. I can listen to new peaceful, sleepy words that can lead me to dreamy, wonderful places."

Let relaxation happen naturally. Let the unconscious part of your brain take over. Let the soft and gentle words carry you further into relaxation. Let the words work their magic. Imagine the words you whisper to yourself coming to life and take you to that peaceful place.

Know those worrying thoughts tell your brain to stay awake as they cause tight sensations in your body and thoughts that repeat again and again in your mind. Imagine them being swept away by your breath as you breathe out, and whatever is left is erased by the kind words you whisper to yourself.

With your worries gone, go ahead now and allow yourself to drift toward peacefulness as you continue to repeat affirmations to become more and more sleepy.

"I cannot relax if I force myself to relax. Instead, I let relaxing words guide me. They can cause my mind and body to relax and deliver me to my peaceful place. My body knows how to breathe. It can do this naturally."

"I can relax and let the kind words bring me back to that peaceful place. I can attain mental tranquility. Rest and relaxation help my body rejuvenate."

Now, as we come to the conclusion of this meditation, I will count down from 10. As I do, feel yourself return to reality.

10… Slowly coming back now…

9…

8…

7… Feel the room around you…

6…

5… Take a deep breath now…

4…

3… Feel your senses returning to your body…

2…

1… And you have returned. You are fully relaxed and energized.

After Work Stress Relieving Meditation (30mns)

Hello and welcome to this after work stress relieving meditation. In this session, we will be working on cleansing both the mind and body from the stress and tension you have accumulated throughout the day.

To begin, make yourself comfortable. You can sit down or lay down, and place your arms however you like so long as you are comfortable. Comfort is important for a productive meditation session.

Go ahead and close your eyes now and focus on your own breathing. Now, take a deep breath to signal to the body that it is time to unwind and relax. Give your body and mind the permission to relax.

Tell yourself that it is important that you relax as much as possible before you sleep tonight. It is important that you get a full, restful sleep so you have the energy to tackle tomorrow's tasks, after all.

You can continue to relax as you listen and breathe. Each time you exhale, you can feel yourself becoming more and more relaxed. More and more relaxed…

Soon, you will experience relaxation and you are probably wondering what that experience will be like.

Rest assured that no matter how deeply relaxed you become, you will remain in complete control. You will stay in control even when you are very deeply immersed in the experience of relaxation.

Now, as you continue to breathe deeply and slowly, you can start to feel yourself becoming more and more relaxed… Eventually, you might even fall asleep, but that is quite alright.

Perhaps you have been working too hard lately so that your body and mind just want to go to sleep. If at any point during this meditation, you want to go to sleep, you may go to bed straight away. After all, the goal of this meditation is to get you to relax, and if you do feel sleepy, then this session is complete.

At the same time, if you feel any discomfort during this session, you may move your body gently to ease that discomfort. Do not let discomfort get in the way of your experience of relaxation.

For a moment, be aware of the normal sounds around you now and whatever you hear from now on will only help to relax you more.

As you exhale, release any tension, any stress from any part of your body your mind, your thoughts just let that stress go.

Just let any stressful thoughts rushing through your mind, feel then begin to wind down…

Wind…

Down…

Wind down and relax…

Begin with letting all the muscles in your face relax, Especially your jaw. Let your teeth part, just a little bit and relax this area. Your jaw and mouth in general are the part where your body is tensest. Most tension and stress gather here.

As such, spend extra time in this area and relax your jaw. Feel that relaxation coming in, going to your temples and relaxing the muscles in your temples. As you think about relaxing, those muscles will just relax. Feel them relax. As you relax, you'll be able to just drift off and float into a deeper and deeper level of total relaxation.

You will continue to relax.

Now, let all of the muscles in your forehead. Relax. Feel those muscles smooth, smooth, and relaxed.

Rest your eyes.

Just imagine that your eyelids are feeling so comfortable, so pleasant, so heavy and so relaxed.

Now, let all the muscles on the back of your neck and shoulders relax as well.

Feel a heavy, heavy weight being lifted off your shoulders and you feel relieved, lighter, and more relaxed.

All of the muscles in the back of your neck and shoulders relax and feel that soothing relaxation.

Go down your back, down, and down, and down to the lower part of your back.

Those muscles just let go with every breath you take and exhale, you're just feeling your body drifting and floating.

Deeper and deeper down…

Deeper down into total relaxation and all that is here now.

Let your muscles go relaxing more and more. Let all of the muscles in your shoulders running down your arms, to your fingertips.

Relax, and let your arms feel so heavy…

So heavy…

So heavy, so comfortable…

So pleasant…

and relaxed…

You may have tingling in your fingertips. That's perfectly fine. You may have warmth in the palms of your hands.

They are so relaxed. they are so heavy, so heavy and so relaxed.

Now, you inhale once again, and relax those chest muscles, and now as you exhale feel your stomach muscles relax.

As you exhale, relax all of the muscles in your stomach. Let them go.

All of the muscles your legs, feel them relax. All of the muscles your legs, so completely relaxed right to the tips of your toes.

You are noticing how very comfortable your body feels.

Just drifting and floating…

Deeper…

Deeper…

Relaxed…

Now, imagine a spreading sense of calm and peace spreading throughout your body. Let go of all of your cares and concerns. Let them drift away like clouds in the wind, dissipating more and more.

Take another deep breath and relax… Let go of your entire body and allow it to be supported by whatever it is that is beneath you. Feel your body loosening up. Shift your focus to the top of your head now and continue to breathe deeply, letting the rejuvenating properties in the air to heal, to loosen, and to relax those areas.

Introduce that healing energy to every single part of your body. Starting from the top of your head, and work your way slowly down toward the tip of your toes. Feel each and every part of your body loosening up and going limb. Feel every single muscle in your body relaxing as you breathe.

Now that your body is entirely at ease, you can start to imagine being somewhere peaceful and relaxing. Perhaps you can picture yourself sunbathing on a quiet beach on a warm sunny day with a beautiful blue sky. But you can imagine being anywhere you like, even in fictional locations. So long as you can feel relaxed and at ease, it is perfect.

That place should be a safe haven for you, somewhere you want to be, or where you can be yourself. You can imagine yourself being there with your mind's eye, and since all the things your body would sense.

This is a safe haven for you, created by the subconscious mind. The magical thing about this place is that it has always been there, in your dreams, but you did not know how to access this place yet. Normally, you can only find this place when you are totally at peace, which usually happens while you are asleep.

Now that you are at total peace, you can access this place again. This time, you can bring it with you to the outside world. That way, when you find yourself stressed or tense, you can simply return to this place through meditation.

Now that you are in your perfect world, take some time to enjoy this place. Sense it with all your senses and take in all its essence so that you may heal and relax even further.

(Pause 1mn)

Inhale deeply and start to close your eyes gently. Relax. And as you are relaxing deeper and deeper, imagine a beautiful staircase leading you to a very peaceful, a very special place for you.

You can imagine it to be any place you choose. Perhaps you would enjoy a beach, or ocean with clean fresh air, or the mountain with a stream and a river. Any place is perfectly fine.

At each breath, you take, imagine you take each step down the staircase and relax even deeper…

(Pause 1mn)

Imagine a peaceful and special place, a place of peacefulness, and soft love. You can imagine this special place and perhaps you can also feel it. Feel the atmosphere here now.

You are here and there is no one to disturb you. Allow yourself to be here now, feeling that sense of peace through you, behind you within you, before you and after you.

Allow this sense of your own special atmosphere of peace and love, this sense of well-being, to stay with you in this space within you, open and alive, long after this session is completed for the rest of this day and evening and tomorrow.

Allow yourself to allow this peace and love to be stronger to come to life, feeling at peace with the sense of wellbeing. Each and every time that you choose to do this kind of relaxation you'll be able to relax deeply and deeper, regardless of the stress and tension that may surround your life.

You are now very deeply relaxed, completely at one with yourself, completely engrossed. Now, focus solely on your special place. Just be there now and know that you are at peace. Calm and relaxed.

There is no tension, no anxiety. Concentrate on this feeling and know that you can take it with you throughout your day tomorrow. No stress or anxiety shall intrude on your mental tranquility. Whenever you are stressed, you can turn to your special place and breathe to allow your body to be calm once more.

Finally, take another deep breath and smile. We are coming to the conclusion of this meditation. Whenever you are ready to go back to reality, simply take another deep breath and open your eyes. For now, you can remain here for as long as you like.

Before Sleep Deep Relaxation Meditation (30mns)

Hello and welcome to this pre-sleep deep relaxation meditation. This meditation is designed to help you relax so you can get a deep, restful sleep. You will wake up the next day feeling energized and fresh.

So to begin, lie down on your bed, find a comfortable resting position, and close your eyes. Find a comfortable position with a spine straight and completely on the mattress. Let's start to check in with yourself here by scanning the physical body, noticing where you're holding tension, noticing where you might feel a lightness or ease.

Scan the emotional body checking in with any feelings of stress that you might be carrying or maybe some emotional lightness or something you're feeling good about.

(Pause 1mn)

Start to check in with your breath noticing where in your body it flows maybe you feel it in the chest. Maybe the belly will notice where it doesn't flow. Maybe the breath is a little shallow.

(Pause 1mn)

Start to deepen the breath, drawing it first into the belly, then the chest, and upper back, and exhaling to release. Another breath into the belly, then the chest, and exhale. Start to slow the breath, holding at the top, and exhale again.

Breathe in… 1, 2, 3.
Pause at the top…
And smooth, even exhale…

Breathing at your own pace. Calm, slow, and smooth. Inhale all the way into the belly, then the chest. Pause for a moment and exhale completely, returning your focus to the physical body. It will start to release some tension, consciously releasing muscles of the face.

As you relax, see if there might have been muscles you didn't even realize you were holding. Relax the throat in the neck, feeling the back of the head sink into the ground fully supported. Relax the shoulders, letting them sink into the ground, relaxing the collarbones, the chest.

Just letting go of the weight that you're carrying. Relax the upper arms, the elbows, the forearms. Relax the hands, letting the fingers come to rest and their natural curl. Still with the breath, smooth inhales. Pausing at the top...

Then exhale, completely releasing the chest, releasing tension across the ribs, letting the middle back and the low back settles onto the ground. Relax the abdomen, relax the hips, and the buttocks, letting them release into the ground.

Relaxing the thighs, the knees, relaxing your calves, and your ankles, staying with the breath as you inhale slowly and smoothly. Pause at the top. Then exhale completely. Relax the feet, relaxing even the toes, letting them fall out to the sides. Slow, smooth inhales.

Check back in with the physical body, noticing if there are still areas where you're keeping the muscle tense, seeing if you can let go a little more, see if you can let go a little more with every exhale, not worrying about where we need to be next or what we might need to do.

Allow yourself this time to intentionally relax.

Take note of any emotional stress just as we do with the physical ones. Exhale them away. smooth long inhales. Pausing at the top. And sending any unwanted stress out with our exhales.

Again, inhale slowly and smoothly... Holding at the top... And exhale...
Allow the mind to rest on the sensation of each breath in and out through the nose.
Check back in with the physical body, noticing where you might be storing tension.

Again, releasing the jaw, releasing the muscles of the face, relaxing shoulders, relaxing the abdomen, the hips, and the legs... Letting the body feel completely supported by the ground beneath you...

Tune into the breath… Notice where in the body the air flows… Notice where it doesn't really reach…

Breathe… The belly, then the chest, and upper back… Then exhale completely… Breathe still with a slow smooth exhale, a pause the top… And release.

Inhale into the belly, then the chest, and then imagine this breath swirling all the way out through the arms and the legs… Inhale, the breath reaching all the way through the body to the fingertips and the toes.

Send this exhale swirling through the ribs and the hips up to your shoulders, imagining this breath coming up the neck into the head even the ears nourished by this inhale, sending fresh oxygen to every place in the body, sending nutrients to yourself intentionally…

Your breath swirls around the entire body, not only does it distribute what you need, it gathers up everything you no longer wish to carry.

Exhale physical tension…

Inhale a new breath… And exhale, releasing emotional stress…

Pause at the bottom before you inhale fresh air sending it all the way out through the body, arms, legs, fingers, toes, hips, shoulders, even your ears, and your nose. Exhale… Releasing any mental chatter, allowing the mind to be fully occupied by sensing as much of the body as you can at one time…

Inhale to nourish… Exhale to release sending out carbon dioxide, sending out physical tension, sending out emotional stress, sending out your mental chatter…

Inhaling clarity a sense of well-being and calm…

Pause at the top before exhaling completely…

Checking in with your breath… Filling first the belly, then the chest, and upper back, before you send this fresh air through the entire body…

Exhale… Checking in with your physical tension, noticing if you holding any tension in the legs or shoulders… and exhaling that tension away. Inhale to fortify, strengthen, and refresh the body… Exhale to let go of all that no longer serves you…

Inhale, filling the belly, then the chest before you send that fresh air to circulate in the entire body… Pause the top and exhale completely, releasing physical tension emotional stress mental chatter on the way out…

Continue these smooth full inhales at an unhurried pace...
Pause at the top and with every exhale, continue to let go...

Staying here on your back, breathing deeply for as long as you'd like and when you're ready to release yourself from this meditation, simply stretch and open your eyes if you wish. Enjoy several unhurried breaths here and smile as you have given yourself the time to relax...
This concludes the deep sleep meditation. Thank you and goodnight.

Guided Meditation for Deep Sleep (30mns)

Hello and welcome to this guided meditation for deep sleep. Here, we will be working on relaxing the mind and body so that you would get a peaceful and restful sleep. That way, you will wake up the next day, feeling totally relaxed, alert, and energized.

So, get comfortable in whatever way you see fit. It is a good idea to lay down or sit right on your bed as you can bring this meditation session to a close by going straight to bed.

Now that you are comfortably settled, go ahead, and close your eyes. If it's more comfortable for you to leave your eyes open, pick a spot that you can stare at without moving your head and focus on that.

Now, take a deep breath, letting your arms hang gently in your shoulder sockets, feeling the tips of your fingers wherever they are. If they're touching your leg, or if they're touching a chair or the floor, notice your arms and fingers hanging gently from your shoulder socket.

Take a slow, gentle breath and feel the air as it passes down your throat. Feel the sides of your chest as they gently expand and with a soft exhale.

On your next breath in, imagine yourself standing at the beach. It is a warm, sunny day and the sky is clear. It is not too hot or cold. The sand feels very fine beneath and you could hear the seagulls in the distance. On the far distance of the beach is a pier. At the end of the pier is a little sailboat and it beckons at you to come closer.

At each breath you take, feel yourself walking slowly toward this boat. As you walk, feel the fine sand beneath your feet. Feel the warm and gentle breeze brushing up against you as you walk. Hear the gentle waves as they come and go. At each breath you take, feel yourself sinking deeper into relaxation.

(Pause 1mn)

You walk up on the pier now and climb into the boat. It looks very cozy and it has a nice little hammock that is just the right size for you. The boat is full of your favorite snacks and drinks. You help yourself to these snacks and drinks as you lie on the hammock, gazing lazily at the sky above.

Taking a deep breath now, you feel the gentle wobble of the boat as it leaves the pier. You feel very safe in this boat and you know that the wind and tide will carry you to where you want to be.

Now, take another deep breath, noticing your jaw muscles as you gently let your breath out so you are standing in the boat you sit down comfortably and as you make yourself comfortable in this little boat.

You notice that the waves are gently rocking you back and forth. You are surrounded by a sense of serenity and calm. Taking a slow deep breath, you feel connected and held in all parts of your life.

At this point, your mind may start to wander and bring up random thoughts that may gladden or upset you. Whatever it is, acknowledge that the thoughts are there and let them go. Simply take a deep breath and return your focus to your place of peace, on the boat.

Continue to enjoy your time on the boat as it sails slowly across the ocean. Here, nothing can harm you. You feel at peace. You feel at ease. You feel very and thoroughly relaxed.

Eventually, you feel that the boat has come to a stop. You stand up and feel that you are exactly where you want to be. It is a place of your wildest dreams. So, take a moment now and imagine this place. Use the power of your imagination, but do not try too hard. The subconscious mind will take over and conjure up such a place that you know is a place of bountiful resources.

(Pause 1mn)

This is a magical spot just for you and you alone. This is the place where you will get everything that your mind and body need to relax and rejuvenate. So, taking a deep breath now, you may start to explore this place. Take your time and use all your senses to sense this place and absorb its magical and relaxing power.

(Pause 1mn)

Inhaling to the top of the belly the middle of the belly you receive all of the trust that you need. Completing your inhale, you receive all of the safety and security that you need. With your exhale, any fear, anger, stress, or discomfort you feel is completely released into the ocean.

In doing so, you receive all of the hope, joy, and peace you need. As you exhale all sadness, loneliness, and grief, fully and gently leave your field. Inhaling into the bottom of your belly, the middle of your belly, and on the top of your belly.

You receive all of the energy that you need, your exhale releases any fatigue, tension, or exhaustion you might be feeling. Take one more breath to receive what you need. If you want to stay here in this place for a few more breaths, feel free to do so.

(Pause 1mn)

Any tension in pain you had noticed before is gone. In fact, you were quite excited and happy that your shoulders are relaxed that your back feels loose straight and strong. You notice that your hips feel open and supported, and all tension in your legs and feet have been released.

You can return to this place of peace and tranquility at any point in the future if you like. All you have to do is to meditate and the door to this place will open for you. You can remain here for as long as you like and feel completely at ease.

Right here, right now, you feel completely safe and relaxed. Nothing can harm you. Everything you need is right here. Nothing in the outside world can harm you. No worldly worries can ruin your peace of mind. So long as you are here, you are safe.

As we come to the end of this meditation, take another deep breath and smile. Smile because you have given yourself the time and space you need to recover and relax. You can remain in this place for as long as you want and you can drift right off to sleep after this session. Thank you and goodnight.

Panic Attack Relaxation meditation (10mns)

Hello and welcome to this guided meditation for relaxation after a panic attack. In this session, we will work toward relaxing the body and mind after a stressful situation.

So, let us begin by getting into a comfortable position. You can lie down or sit and place your arms and legs however you like so long as you are comfortable. If you haven't done so already, go ahead and close your eyes. As your vision fades to black, shift your focus to your breathing.

Relax…

Take a deep breath in and slowly release it.

Continue these deep breaths, making sure to fill your lungs completely and breathe deep into your belly.

As you breathe in, feel the positive energy flowing into your body.

As you breathe out, visualize the negative energy, stress, and worries flowing out of you.

Continue to breathe this way for a few more minutes to allow the body and mind to slow down, unwind, and relax…

(Pause 3mns)

At this point, your mind may start to wander. It might bring up worrying thoughts, some of which may be caused by the panic attack you just experienced. If that is the case, simply push those thoughts aside and focus on your breathing. Use it as an anchor to hold your focus in the present moment.

Right now, there is nothing else you need to do but to unwind and relax. Unwind… And relax…

Take another deep breath to help the body relax. If your mind wanders, gently guide your focus back to your breathing.

And as you are relaxing deeper and deeper, imagine a beautiful staircase leading you to a very peaceful, a very special place for you.

You can imagine it to be any place you choose. Perhaps you would enjoy a beach, or ocean with clean fresh air, or the mountain with a stream and a river. Any place is perfectly fine.

At each breath, you take, imagine you take each step down the staircase and relax even deeper…

(Pause 1mn)

Imagine a peaceful and special place, a place of peacefulness, and soft love. You can imagine this special place and perhaps you can also feel it. Feel the atmosphere here now.

You are here and there is no one to disturb you. Allow yourself to be here now, feeling that sense of peace through you, behind you within you, before you and after you.

Allow this sense of your own special atmosphere of peace and love, this sense of well-being, to stay with you in this space within you, open and alive, long after this session is completed for the rest of this day and evening and tomorrow.

Allow yourself to allow this peace and love to be stronger to come to life, feeling at peace with the sense of wellbeing.

Each and every time that you choose to do this kind of relaxation you'll be able to relax deeply and deeper, regardless of the stress and tension that may surround your life.

You may now also remain in this peace calmer, more relaxed, allowing the tensions and stresses to bounce off and away from you…

Just bouncing off

And away from you…

And allowing this deeper sense of who you are to stay with you, growing stronger and stronger throughout the day.

As we come to the conclusion of this meditation, you can spend as much time in this place. And whenever you decide to leave, know that you can bring this place and its calming aura with you to the outside world. Whenever you feel stressed again, simply meditate once more and imagine this place.

It will take you back here and you can be free from the worldly worries again until you are ready to return. Again, remain here for as long as you like. When you are ready, simply take a deep breath and slowly open your eyes.

Thank you.

Morning Mood Booster Meditation (10mns)

Hello and welcome to this morning mood booster meditation. You've just woken up and felt ready for the day ahead, but your body and mind may not be ready. Meditation as a means to transition between a relaxed state to an alert state is recommended to start off your day right.

In this session, we will work toward calming the mind and body and bringing in more energy to them. Through the power of breathing alone, we will work toward bringing the springs back into your steps At the end of this session, you will feel refreshed and alert.

So without further ado, let's get started.

Begin by getting into a comfortable position, be it laying down or sitting up in a brightly lit and open area. Perhaps on the couch in your living room or the front or back yard. Just make sure that the place is quiet because we do not want to overwhelm the mind with stimulants too soon.

Once you are nicely settled in, take a deep breath to tell your body that it is time to wake up and prepare for the day ahead, which may be full of chaos and stress. But you need not worry about that right now.

Take another deep breath in through your nose, and let it flow out through your mouth...

In... And out...
In... And out...
In... And out...

Excellent. If your eyes are still open, go ahead and close them now. As your vision fades to black, shift your focus to your own breathing. Continue to breathe like this for another minute.

(Pause 1mn)

At this point, your mind may start to wander. It might bring up random thoughts that make you feel a certain way. Right now is the time to bring in energy to the mind and body. So, if your mind does wander, simply disregard them and focus back on your breathing.

The body and mind are very resilient. Only through imaginable and harsh circumstances can one hope to break them. So long as you are taking the time to care for your body and mind, nothing can break them and you will come back home at the end of the day, still feeling like you have some energy left to spend with your loved one and pursue your passion.

Perhaps you care for your pets or ride very carefully. For your pets, you might make sure that they are well fed and have enough toys and water while you are out at work. If you own a car, you might make sure that it has enough gas, and the engine is well taken care of. You might take care of your possessions carefully.

Now, you choose to take care of yourself. You chose to take care of yourself as if your body is your most valuable possession, which is true. Your body and mind are your most valuable possessions and you now choose to treat them with the value they deserve. This is a very precious gift to give yourself.

Take another deep breath now and smile because you have decided to give yourself a very beautiful gift. In doing so, you choose to acknowledge how valuable you really are. Maybe you have treated yourself too harshly. Maybe you did not treat yourself in a kind and gentle way.

So now take the time to give yourself love and relaxation. The day ahead might be full of chaos. It might be full of stress. But in knowing that you are well taken care of, you are alright.

So as we come to the conclusion of this meditation, you can take some time and enjoy this stillness, this calm, this tranquility. Whenever you are ready to move on, simply take a deep breath, open your eyes, and you may go on with your day.

Thank you and have a good day.

Lunchtime Relaxation Meditation (15mns)

Hello and welcome to this lunchtime relaxation meditation. It is currently midday and you still have many hours to go before your day ends. But the fact that you are here means that either your body and mind are tired already or that you simply want to take some time off to rejuvenate even though you can still get through the day just fine.

Regardless, we will work toward relaxing the body and mind and bring energy back to them so that you can continue to maintain your peak performance. So go ahead now and get into a comfortable position and get ready to meditate. Make sure that you are in a distraction-free area so you can meditate in peace.

It does not matter how you sit or lay down. Place your arms and legs however you like so long as you are comfortable. Comfort is of utmost importance for a productive meditation session, after all.

Once you are ready, take a deep breath and close your eyes. When your vision fades to black, shift your focus to your own breathing. We will be using this breathing to bring in the energy that your body needs.

So go ahead and take a deep breath now and enjoy the relaxation and energy it brings.

On your next breath in, I want you to take a deep breath through your nose and hold it at the top for 3 seconds before exhaling through your mouth. As you hold your breath, focus on the stillness.

So go ahead and take a deep breath in through your nose…
Hold it for a few seconds… Focusing on the stillness…
And exhale slowly…

As you continue to breathe this way, feel how the air flows in and out of your body. Feel the stillness in your body when you hold your breath. Continue to breathe this way for a minute.

(Pause 1mn)

At this point, your mind may start to wander. After working for some time, the mind may not have calmed down yet and it will continue to bring up random thoughts. Some of them might be about the work you will soon return to. Some of them might be about other worries that you have for the future.

Whatever those thoughts are, set them aside for now. There is plenty of time to worry but now is not that time. Simply acknowledge that you might be worried about somethings but then push those thoughts away and shift your focus back to your breathing.

Right now, you may allow your breath to return to its natural rhythm. As you continue to breathe, imagine that the air you bring into your body having that bright glow. It is the healing energy that the air carries. By breathing in deeply of that air, you are bringing that healing energy into your body.

Your body will take that energy and heal itself. It will take that energy and use it to power itself so that it may continue to function at its best throughout the day. At the same time, as you breathe out, you are using the air to dispel any negativity or stress or tension from your body.

Continue to breathe and allow your body to absorb this positive energy for a while.

(Pause 2mns)

As we come to the end of this meditation, you may continue to remain in your meditative position. Whenever you are ready to return to work again, take a deep breath and smile. Thank yourself for allowing you to take a moment to relax and rejuvenate. Thank you for allowing you to enjoy this positive. Give yourself a pat on the back and open your eyes.

Thank you and have a nice day.

Quick Anxiety Reducing Meditation (15mns)

Hello and welcome to this quick anxiety-reducing meditation. In this session, you will embark on a journey to relaxation, away from the worries of the outside world. In this place, your peaceful place, you will experience a wonderful calmness and meditative state of mind.

To begin, get into a comfortable position be it sitting or lying down. You may place your arms and legs however you want so long as you are comfortable. Comfort is of utmost importance after all and it is crucial for your relaxation.

So, go ahead now and take a deep breath, telling your body and mind that it is time to unwind and relax. This time is for you and you alone. There is nothing else you need to do at this point.

If you haven't done so already, go ahead and close your eyes now. As your vision fades to black, shift your focus to your breathing. We will use the power of breathing to calm both the mind and body down.

On your next breath, allow the air to flow in through your nose, but hold your breath for a few seconds before your exhale. Focus on the gentle stillness between your inhale and exhale. Continue to breathe this way for a while and study the essence of this gentle stillness in the air.

(Pause 1mn)

Now, let us work on relaxing the body. To do so, simply shift your focus to the top of your head and slowly move it down to the rest of your body. Starting with the forehead now, focus on that area, and introduce that stillness to your forehead. Allow the muscles to return to their natural position. Feel them soften and relax.

Going down slowly to your brows now… Take that stillness and let your brows absorb that relaxation from your breathing… Introduce that relaxation to your eyelids, nose, cheeks, lips, tongue, and jaw…

Feel tour entire head relaxing and become light as all worries are washed away, yet heavy with the aura of relaxation… Bring that peace and relaxation to your torso now, and feel it loosening up and relaxing just as I say the word "Relax"…

So… Relax… Unwind and relax… Deeper and deeper now…

Bring that relaxing aura to your limbs… Arms and legs… Let all muscles return tot heir natural position, where they can unwind and relax… Take another deep breath now and feel your fingers and toes returning to their natural positions, light and free from worries, yet heavy from relaxation…

Feel your body becoming loose and limp, free from stress, and full of relaxation… Take another deep breath to tell the body and mind to relax, to rejuvenate, to release all that tension…

You are completely in control of this meditation session, so you can return to your awakened state whenever you wish. You can do so by just opening your eyes once more.

Now, breathe in deeply and exhale fully.

Breathe in deeply…

And exhale fully…

Allow the sound of your breathing to soothe and calm your mind and soul.

Breathe in deeply…

And exhale fully…

At this point, your mind may start to wander. It might bring up some random thoughts, some are happy, some are worrying, some are sad, some that caused you so much anxiety.

This is fine. This is completely normal. Simply acknowledge that such thoughts exist and tell yourself that you will address all of those problems after this session. Just by doing this, those thoughts will begin to quiet down as you concentrate on listening to your own breathing.

As you listen to your inhale, you will find your mind gently begin to quiet down.

So, breathe in deeply, taking in the cool and refreshing air

And exhale fully, pushing out hot and tense air.

You may feel your body starting to loosen up and relaxing as you allow the sound of your own breathing to soothe your soul, taking in the infinite source of energy within you.

Just through breathing alone, you allow yourself to be in total peace with your surroundings.

Allow the sound of your breathing to continue relaxing your whole body, and take your time to enjoy this wonderful experience. You can remain in this deeply relaxed state for a while and smile as you now have completed this meditation session. You can now have a restful sleep.

Guided Self-Healing Meditation (30mns)

Hello and welcome to this guided self-healing meditation. In this session, we will work on soothing the pain and tension in your body. At the end of this session, you will feel very liberated, free from all that stress and negative energy.

So without further ado, let us get started. Simply get into a comfortable position. You can sit or lie down, whatever works for you as long as you are comfortable. It is important that you can relax so you can effectively heal your body.

If you haven't already, go ahead and close your eyes. As your vision fades to black, shift your focus to your breathing. Take a deep breath now to tell the body that it is time to unwind and relax.

Right now, there is nothing else you need to do but to relax and enjoy the relaxation. Right now is the time to relax, rejuvenate, and regain your strength. If at any moment during this meditation, you feel that any part of your body is becoming uncomfortable, you may shift slightly to ease that discomfort.

Now, let us work on soothing the body, encouraging healing energy to move to the places within the body where it is most required. Those places can focus more deeply on repairing and healing themselves, feeling stronger and healthier.

Now, take another deep breath and feel your upper torso expanding and contracting gently as you breathe. In through the nose and out through the mouth, continue to breathe this way for a while.

(Pause 2mns)

At this point, your mind may start to wander and bring up random thoughts. Right now is not the time to worry, so gently guide your focus back to your breathing. Tell yourself that you will return to address those thoughts at a later date.

As you breathe deep and slow, focus all your attention on the breath. You can focus on how the air moves into your nose, passes your throat, and fills up your lungs or stomach. Make sure to give yourself a natural pause between the inhalation and the exhalation for the best experience.

Now, take a deep breath in…
And out…

At this point, you may allow your breathing to return to its natural rhythm. Your body will find the right rhythm on its own. You may notice that, at each breath you take, you are becoming more relaxed. With each exhale, imagine the tension in your body flying right out.

With each inhale, imagine breathing in deep relaxation, feeling more peaceful, more calm, more centered, with every breath.

Now, picture yourself standing close to a river, which is poured forth by a magnificent waterfall high above. You are in the middle of a forest. It is sunny and the sky is clear. It is not too hot or too cold.

In fact, though you are in the middle of, what seems to you, nowhere, you feel very much at ease. Somehow, this place feels very familiar and you do not know exactly where you are... Not just yet.

You sit down at the base of a tall tree, its leaves provide cool shades from the sun. You lay there, your back against the tree and your bottom supported by the soft and cool soil beneath. You let go of your body, feeling very relaxed and safe.

So while you are here, enjoy your time in this very beautiful and peaceful place. Sense this magical place with all your senses. Hear the cries of the wildlife that sang, only adding more to your relaxation. Listen to the water crashing down from the waterfall, its torrent flowing as true as your breathing. Take a few minutes now to enjoy your time in this place.

(Pause 3mns)

With the next exhale, let go. Let go. Allow the relaxation to happen to you, inviting it in of new your arms up to it welcoming it. It's so nice to be relaxed and it's so nice to even increase that relaxation by doubling it or tripling it and notice now how much extra relaxation you like at this very moment and breathing in.

As you breathe out, allowing that extra relaxation doubling or tripling it, to move through the body. Calm and relaxed. Soft and peaceful.

All the focus on letting go. The sound of my voice, nothing at all to do. Just follow the sound of my voice.

Very soon, we will work on melting away all the pain and soften the stiff muscles in your body. We will bring in the energy into all the right places, to direct it as you are in charge of your body. It can direct the healing energy wherever its most needed.

So let us begin by imagining that the air contains some healing properties. Let us give it a color, a vivid and radiant yellow, a symbol of positivity. Focus on its radiant beauty, its healing essence, and feel your body glow in this yellow at each breath you take. All that beautiful color, full of healing energy, full of tenderness, full of hope, full of prosperity.

Allow that color to move down into the body all the way down to a chest to the stomach so it sits in the core of the body and it radiates outwards. Perhaps it glows. Perhaps it vibrates.

Allow that healing energy a healing color to stay right there and yet it is becoming stronger and brighter and more powerful. Now, allow the mind to scan the whole body and find any spot where healing is required.

Moving your focus gently down your body from the top of your head to the tips of your toes now, finding any areas where your body is tense or stressed. But do not scrutinize. Allow your mind to guide you to that spot as the mind knows the body well, and the body also knows the mind well. Allow them to guide you on this healing process as they know what they need.

The mind will take you to those parts in the body that are damaged and are in pain that needs healing, some more than others. Find that first place and just watch. Just watch it through the mind's eye and notice the color, the shape, and you might notice that the area is more rigid. Perhaps more solid. It could be a block. Perhaps it's a bottleneck.

Whatever that tense area may feel or look like, when you finally find it, take a deep breath in. As you do so, feel that positive healing energy flowing into your body. Allow that energy to soak up in that tense area and erasing any signs of tension. Allow this radiant healing power to soothe that pain, that tension, or that stress. As you breathe out, feel the air that you exhale carrying away all that stress from your body, just like the flow of the river.

Continue to introduce this healing energy to the rest of your body until you are completely comfortable.

(Pause 2mns)

Now, it is time to finally relax the body thoroughly. On your next breath, feel your body absorbing all that healing positive energy. Imagine that your body is soaking up all that energy like a sponge and your body is glowing brighter and brighter, more radiant, more powerful. As you continue to breathe, feel your body sinking deeper and deeper into the state of relaxation.

You can repeat this process anywhere in the body by melting away the pain by bringing in that healing color, that loving energy, and making everything better, turning on all the cells in the area to heal and regenerate allowing that own pain to disappear permanently.

Just breathe in and out in a gentle rhythm as you do so.

(Pause 1 minute)

Your whole body now calm and relaxed. A beautiful peacefulness having flowed all through the body, through every muscle, and all old tension now has disappeared and that lovely and healing energy can fill the whole of the body.

Now, feel that energy flowing from the top of your head all the way to the tips of your toes. Feel this healing light radiating through your body. Feel this energy going through your legs and the hips, healing wounds all the way. From the shoulders to the arms, to the very tips of the fingers, through the whole of the chest and the neck, right up to the edge.

All in all, everything just gets better and better every day in every single way, healing and becoming stronger every day getting better and better as you care for yourself or look after yourself as you encourage this healing energy to flow to all the right places within you as you direct it.

As we come to the end of this meditation, picture yourself standing up again and gaze around at the magical place that you have been spending the last several minutes at.

Did you know that this is a place that your subconscious mind created? It knows exactly what is needed for you to heal. It knows exactly what your body and mind need. Now that you have visited this place consciously, you can return to this place again in the future.

All you have to do is to meditate and you will be transported back here, where nothing can harm your peace of mind.

Now, to conclude this meditation, I will count down from 5. As I do so, you will feel yourself returning to reality. Let us begin.

5… Slowly coming back now…

4… Feel your consciousness returning to your body…

3… Wiggle your toes now…

2… Take a deep breath…

1… Slowly open your eyes.

This concludes this meditation session. Thank you and have a nice day.

Easy to Follow Self-Healing Meditation (20mns)

Hello and welcome to this self-healing meditation. In this session, we will be working toward easing the pain and tension inside the body and allow you to rest comfortably. Self-healing meditation goes beyond just healing the body, but also the kind as well. If you are feeling hopeless, depressed, or stuck in a state of pain, then this quick self-healing meditation can help you shift your mindset to a more positive place.

First, get into a comfortable position, be it sitting or laying down. You may place your arms and legs however you like so long as you are comfortable. You will be here for quite a while, after all. As this meditation is intended to ease any tension within the body and mind, it pays to remain in a comfortable position.

If at any point in this session, you feel any discomfort from staying still, you may move a bit to ease that pain and you can return to this meditation seamlessly.

Right now, you don't have to close your eyes yet. You don't have to focus on anything. Just let the mind go about on its business and your eyes gazing at random things in your room.

Right now, you just want to tell the body and mind to relax. So go ahead and take a deep breath to let the body and mind know that it is time to unwind. Take another deep breath now and allow yourself to sink further into the state of relaxation.

In… And out…
In… And out…
In… And out…

Excellent. If you haven't done so already, go ahead and close your eyes now. Slowly do so and let your vision fade to black. Inhale deeply and exhale completely. Allow your body to relax and to be still. Let your muscles soften and let your muscles lengthen.

On your next breath, breathe in through your nose, hold it at the top for a few seconds and then exhale slowly. As you hold your breath, focus on the stillness in the air and your body and mind. Focus on what that stillness feels like.

Remember what it feels like as we will spread its tranquility toward the rest of the body and mind.

Now, let us work on relaxing the body. We will do a simple body scan exercise. Simply shift your focus from your breathing to the top of your head, and move it slowly down your body until you reach the tips of your toes.

As you do so, notice any sensations that you feel. Gently pay attention. Some areas may already be relaxed. Some might be tense. If you notice any areas of tension or discomfort, simply take notice of where they are as we will come back to them later.

Let go of any judgment. Just be aware and sensitive to the messages of your body. Now bring your focus to your breathing. Notice the depth and notice the pace of every inhale and every exhale, allow your breath to become slower and softer.

Take a deep inhale through your nose and a long exhale through your mouth. Try that again. Deep inhale through your nose… And long exhale through your mouth.

Feel every breath flowing through your body as you inhale and as you exhale, stay connected to the sensations of your body.

At this point, your mind may start to wander and bring up random thoughts. Some of them might be worrying. Some are pleasant. Whatever those thoughts are, simply acknowledge their presence. Maybe you could remain with them for a few seconds, but no longer. Push them aside and guide your focus back to your breathing, using it to anchor yourself to the present moment.

Now, give your body permission to relax and to let go breathe in love and breathe out tension. Breathe in peace and breathe out negativity. Breathe and healing, breathe out hurt. Stay focused on this breath.

Allow your body to soften breathe in love, breathe out tension.

Using your breath as an anchor, focus on that stillness between your inhale and exhale. Observe it and understand its power. Use the healing power of your breathing and introduce that stillness to any part of the body that is hurt or tense.

Scan through your body once more and when you find that area of tension, focus on that area, and breathe deeply and intensely. Allow the breath to sweep away that tension like a gentle yet powerful tide that takes all the negative energy from your body.

Continue to do this for a few minutes or until your body is thoroughly relaxed.

(Pause 3mns)

Now let us work on cleansing the mind of that negative energy. As you breathe, introduce all that positive energy to the mind. Breathe in positivity, breathe out negativity.

Breathe in rejuvenation, breathe out tension.

Breathe in self-love, breathe out self-loathing.

Breathe in love, breathe out stress.

Breathe in peace, breathe out chaos.

Allow your body to be still and to be silent. Let your body and mind do the job. All you have to do is breathe deeply. They will do the rest. They will heal what needs to be healed.

With every breath, allow yourself to relax further and deeper. Allow this feeling of relaxation and calm to spread throughout your whole body feel the sense of peace wash over you.

Be here right now. Every cell in your body knows how to heal itself your body is always working towards perfect health.

Choose to release any and all obstacles to healing, choose to wash your thinking, and think only healthy, loving thoughts. Choose to love your body and send love to every organ, bone, muscle, and part of your body.

Now flood every cell of your body with love. Choose to be grateful to your body. Choose to accept healing and good health.

Now take a deep breath. This concludes this healing meditation.

Guided Sleep Meditation (20mns)

Hello and welcome to this guided sleep meditation. In this session, you will go on a journey of deep relaxation after a long day of work when you just want to unwind and have a restful sleep.

To begin, make sure that all distractions are as minimal as possible. As you progress, anything holding you back from fully relaxing will slowly start to fade away. Lay in a position that is comfortable for you. Allow yourself to go deeper and experience a willing openness to the sleep that you should be getting.

Please leave all thoughts about yourself behind and anything that has caused worry or stress. It may be easier said than done but just place it to the back of your mind for now.

Focus on my voice and the words that you hear will give clarity to unfold your mind for sleep.

If you are ready and willing to be present at this moment, your journey into a deep relaxing and pleasing sleep will begin.

As you lay there in a gentler awareness of observation, noticing how your body is laid, sense, and feel any areas soften to a looseness that promotes a sleepier state.

Now, breathe in deeply and exhale fully.

Breathe in deeply…

And exhale fully…

Allow the sound of your breathing to soothe and calm your mind and soul.

Breathe in deeply…

And exhale fully…

You may notice that thoughts and internal mental chatters are happening inside your mind.

This is fine.

This is completely normal.

These thoughts will begin to quiet down as you concentrate on listening to your own breathing.

As you listen to your inhale, you will find your mind gently begin to quiet down.

So, breathe in deeply, taking in the cool and refreshing air

And exhale fully, pushing out hot and tense air.

You may feel your body starting to loosen up and relaxing as you allow the sound of your own breathing to soothe your soul, taking in the infinite source of energy within you.

Just through breathing alone, you allow yourself to be in total peace with your surroundings.

Now, take the time to scan your entire body, noticing any areas of tension. Focus your breathing on those areas, starting from your toes and moving up to the top of your head. Work on one area at a time.

Breathe deep and slow, allowing your breath to soothe any tension in your muscles.

(Pause 5mns)

Now that your entire body is fully relaxed, take another breath to allow your body to slip more and more into a relaxed state.

Feel how at ease your mind and body are. Feel the relief and benefit of letting go of any worries that were on your thoughts...

Going into an even deeper, sleepier, and more relaxed state, let the visualization of any thoughts begin to fade off in the darkness behind your eyelids, drifting deeper into a transitioning positive dream and sleep...

As you sleep, your body rests, healing as you recuperate and regenerate positive energy in every muscle fiber and cell of yourself.

Sleeping keeps your mind and body muscle memory to remember that when you sleep well, you can do it again. Let go of anything holding you back and truly allow yourself to relax through letting go.

Your mind has the space to rationalize every thought to a groundedness of truth and ones that only benefits you as the person you are on the inside.

Allow yourself to be more at ease with each and every thought that passes your mind. Any tension from this moment on that is caused by our worry or a stressor in your life is quickly brought to a reasonable place. See it for what it truly is before manifesting itself in your body.

You are not the manifestation of such worrying thoughts, so dismiss them with positive self-love that only nourishes your mind and body better.

As you begin and continue to let go of anything negative, you will find that you become more relaxed, calmer, and more at peace within everything.

Going deeper every muscle now, descending more as you slip into an even sleepier state. Knowing that you have more control over how you reason with your mind allows you to go deeper, no sound from the outside can be heard, no light except the positivity inside you that shines, and a feeling of touch is but now a softness of comfort.

Resting, heavily breathing deeply, you just let go. The touch of the sheets beneath you begin to fade away. The sensation of your own vibrations and internal energy are the only things you can sense.

Everything is being replaced with a positive and healing feeling of peace inside. There is no need to think about anything right now. Now is a time for sleep and only sleep. It's the one thing that will replenish you every night as you lay there.

Feel the vibration of positivity growth around your whole body. You may see it as a distant colored light behind your eyelids or a feeling of tingling in your hands or toes, warmer and heavier with each and every noticeably relaxing breath that you take, every inhalation of oxygen only sends you deeper into a space of contentedness and peace. The sense of relief is immense and far-reaching into the deep thoughts of your mind.

Healing any bad feeling you have of yourself. Only positive thoughts can be experienced in this moment and every moment onwards allowing you to drift heavier and warmly into it refreshing deep sleep.

As you sleep the defense mechanism only grows to protect you from negativity. You feel it as a glowy warm feeling around your heart or chest area, growing in strength as you sleep, feeling more positive with every second that passes.

From this moment on you only sleep a positive sleep. You only rest and relax more easily and from this moment on, you find it easier to drift off, feeling the relief of letting go of every aspect of today, leaving it all behind to be nourished and filled with only positivity in every sense of your inner being.

Rest now. Relax more, and just let go.

Stress Relief Meditation (30mns)

Hello and welcome to this stress relief meditation. This meditation is designed to help you relax and be as calm as you can. So go ahead and get into a comfortable position, be it sitting or laying down. Whatever works for you so long as you are comfortable, which is important for a fruitful meditation session.

Next, take a deep breath. You do not even have to close your eyes or focus on anything in particular. You can let your eyes and mind roam as much as they please. For now, all you have to do is to just breathe deeply and let your body and mind unwind and relax.

Breathe in… And out…
In… and out…
In... And out…

Excellent. Now, when you inhale, slowly close your eyes and open them again as you exhale. Continue to do this for a minute or so or until your eyes become heavy. If they do become heavy, you may go ahead and close them.

(Pause 1mn)

Good. Your eyes should start to feel very heavy right now, so go ahead and close them if you haven't already and shift your focus to your breathing.

As you continue to breathe, observe how it feels, how the air enters and exits your body. Study how the air flows throughout your body in all its essence.

(Pause 1mn)

On your next breath in, take a deep breath through your nose and hold it at the top for a few seconds before you let it out through the mouth. This time, focus on that gentle stillness in the air as you hold your breath. Again, observe what it feels like and all of its essence. Continue to do this for another minute or so.

(Pause 1mn)

Excellent. Now, you may allow your breath to return to its natural rhythm. As you listen to my voice, your body may begin to relax more and more. Trust that your body can find its best way to let go naturally. You cannot force relaxation.

Maybe that your body needs to heal in other ways. It's good to know that your unconscious mind is an expert in healing and balancing in a safe and natural way while you can just flow with the experience.

Now, take a few deep breaths…
In… And out…
Continue to do this until your body sinks deeper into relaxation.

(Pause 1mn)

Become aware of your breathing. Imagine now that you're breathing in that life energy through the soles of your feet, breathing it up through your body, and breathe it out the top of your head. Continue to breathe and feel this flow of energy…

(Pause 1mn)

There is no right the wrong way to flow with this experience. Just breathe and relax, feeling the life energy flowing through you…

(Pause 2mns)

Feel the deep sense of comfort as you breathe…

(Pause 1mn)

If at any point during this session, your mind starts to wander, simply guide it back to your breathing. No need to beat yourself up for it because it is natural for the mind to wander and bring up random thoughts sometimes.

There is no need to stress about it. Just acknowledge that the thought is there and tell yourself that you will return to address those thoughts at a later time. Tell yourself that now is the time to relax, not stress about anything. There is a time and place for everything and right here, right now is not the time to feel any negativity. Now is the time for self-care and self-love, that which you truly deserve.

As you acknowledge this fact, you might already be starting to chip away any worry, fear, and stress in the subconscious mind. This will continue with every second in every minute of every breath.

Now, imagine yourself walking on a warm beach. Imagine walking so close to the sea that some of the waves touch your feet. As the waves come crashing in on the shore, synchronize your breath with them. The waves coming in is your inhaling, and the waves fading out back to sea as you exhale. Feel the waves washing away your troubled thoughts.

This is your safe haven. This is a beautiful place formed by the power of the subconscious mind. It knows that this place brings relaxation to the body and mind and it created that just for you.

As you wander this place, know that this is your safe place. It is safe for you to let go of all your worldly worries. Now, picture the sun above you glowing bright yet emit a gentle healing aura and bathing your body with its divine power. Feel yourself glowing with this radiant light, feel its energy surging through your body, and filling you with a peaceful silence.

This quietness flows through your veins permeating every cell in your body.

Feel every atom every molecule of your body, mind, and spirit allowing yourself to be healed and balanced, becoming very aware of that deep sense of peacefulness inside you.

As you do so and I'll leave you in silence for a few moments as your body, mind, heart, and spirit continue the process of letting go and heal.

(Pause 2mn)

Now, you are calm. You feel calm and balanced. This sense of calm, control and balance will continue to grow stronger and stronger every day, more and more, as you meditate and reinforce these positive energies within you.

You're doing good. You are taking control of your mind, body, and emotions. You are feeling better and better, feeling calm, harmonious, and relaxed at all times.

That calmness, that inner peace is growing and spreading through and around your body. As you continue to relax the things in life that were not giving you a positive experience now, they seem to calm you now.

They seem to make you stronger now. They seem to connect you with your inner strengths and power.

Whatever you experience in life, you are better than that. You choose to show up in your life and honor the opportunity that you have been given.

You are a pure life force in the human body. You are worthy

Imagine that you start walking forwards along the beach leaving footprints in the sand the Sun still beaming its powerful celestial energy upon your being.

You feel surprisingly freer. Imagine that every step every footprint represents patterns that are not supportive of your intention to live your full potential and it is safe for you to let go now so you walk steadily and courageously towards your new future.

After a while, you turn around maybe you notice that your footprints are being washed away by the waves. Your first steps are gone now washed away

Let go now and it is safe and you're doing good. For each step you take, the lighter and freer you feel walking more and more effortlessly towards your new future much freer.

Ahead of you, there is a person approaching. It is you. It is you one month from now.

Notice how relaxed your future self feels. Notice how good your future self feels that balanced energy is emanating from your future self over there.

Your future self comes towards you and gives you the warmest most compassionate hug that you have felt in a long time. All that love unconditionally flowing between you. The effect of this positivity will be reinforced in your dreams, compounded in your sleep. You'll wake up tomorrow feeling marvelous, looking forward to another great day in your life.

You feel confident to do all the things you want to do it's getting easier and easier and situations that used to bother you now just seemed to make you stronger.

They seem to connect you with your inner power and it's getting easier and easier.

You feel calm, strong, confident, and relaxed each day as you become increasingly more able to let go and relax so you feel a sense of calmness, a sense of peacefulness growing inside you.

This growing feeling of inner calmness, quiet, confidence, is sufficient to reassure you that as each day passes, you are more and more becoming the person you'd like to be. The ideal for you. The authentic you. You are worthy. You are a believer in yourself. You're more than good enough. You are valuable.

You are important. You are worthy. You're more than good enough. You are courageous and you stand up for yourself because you choose to be you. You are flexible to changes happening in your life.

The more accepting you are to change, the easier it feels. Change is a natural aspect of life. It is a sign of life and you choose life.

You are a beautiful expression of life. You breathe easily in a relaxed way and you detach more and more from the earthly drama that's going on around us.

You can begin to experience a greater and greater sense of joy in your life now and as each day passes, you become happier healthier, and more fulfilled and totally at ease in yourself.

You are safe. You accept that you are you.

All these words are vibrating at the frequency of truth and because all of this begin to happen now.

You begin to feel much happier much more content, much more optimistic, much more positive in every way. You radiate goodness. The future you and then now you embrace one more time this time becoming one.

When you feel ready and decide to open your eyes you will bring with you this positive radiant energy that emanates from within you. Your inner light shines stronger and brighter than ever.

You may be surprised by how calm strong and content you feel in the hours days weeks and months ahead. All is well.

Calming After a Panic Attack Meditation (20mns)

Hello and welcome to this guided calming meditation. In this session, we will be working toward relaxing the mind and body. The fact that you are here means that you had just gone through a rather unfortunate and stressful situation. We will work to repair the damage that the event has caused so that you may return to your day, feeling better.

So, go ahead and get into a comfortable position, be it laying down or sitting up. We will be here for a while, so you want to be as comfortable as possible. During this session, if you ever feel any discomfort, you may move your body a bit to ease that discomfort.

Without further ado, close your eyes if you haven't already. As you do so, focus on your breathing, how the air enters and exits your body. Take a deep breath to tell the body and mind that it is time to slow down, to tell them that there is no need to go anywhere or think about anything.

Tell yourself that you are right where you want to be. Now is the time to unwind and relax. You are safe here. Nothing can harm you here. Nothing can take away the inner peace and tranquility within you. So take another deep breath now and let that peace and tranquility seep out of your subconscious mind, and bathing the body and mind with its magical aura.

Take a deep breath in through your nose, holding it at the top for 2 or 3 seconds, and then breathe out through your mouth. As you do so, focus on that gentle stillness between your inhale and exhale. Observe it in all its essence and introduce it to every inch of your being. Allow this gentle stillness or peace to soothe and calm the body and mind.

Remain with your breath and breathe like this for a few minutes.

(Pause 3mns)

Excellent. You may continue to breathe as you normally would now. At this point, your mind may start to wander and it might randomly bring up various thoughts that make you feel different things. It might bring up pleasant thoughts, which may make you smile. It might bring up unpleasant thoughts, which may displease you. Some negative thoughts might be about the things that caused you so much distress in the first place.

Right now is not the time to think, so if your mind does wander, simply guide it back to your breathing, using your breath as an anchor to hold it in the present moment. Focus on the stillness in the air and the gentle flow of your breathing.

Relax…

Nothing here can harm you…

All will be well…

Things might look bad for you, but if you return to it with a clear head, you can solve any problem. Nothing is impossible. Just give your body and mind enough time and space and they will help you achieve your purpose…

Maybe you are worrying too much. Maybe you are trying to control things that are completely out of your control. Maybe luck just wasn't in your favor.

Whatever the case may be, the fact that you felt the way you did was valid. All feelings are valid and you need to acknowledge that. But remaining in that stressful situation is not the way to go. You need to have a clear mind so that you can make the right decisions and make the best out of the situation.

To do this, you need to relax… Unwind and relax… Take a deep breath now to remind your body and mind to relax. Right now is not the time for worry. You will come back to your duties at a later time.

Without moving your body, surrender everything to the universe around you. Let go of everything and let the universe support your entire being. Unwind and let go, allowing the surface beneath you to support your body.

Welcome the universe with open arms and tell yourself that the universe is kind and loving. If it is not kind and loving, why do such things feel so pleasant in the first place? You are a child of the universe, and the universe loves you just like a loving parent would.

It is not here to harm you. It is here to heal you. Simply let go and welcome its presence with open arms. Allow it to hold you, to cradle you, to give you positivity. Things may not go the way you want them to, but that might be because the universe got something even better planned for you. Trust in the universe and you can never go wrong.

Take a moment now and smile to yourself, for you chose to go through this session and experience the love that grows within you as we speak. Thank yourself for giving yourself time and space to unwind and relax, so that you can go back out there with a clear head and a calm mind.

As we come to the end of this session, take another deep breath and open your eyes whenever you are ready to take on the world once more. With the entire universe behind your back, all your endeavors will succeed.

Thank you and good luck with your journey.

Deep Relaxation Meditation (20mns)

Hello and welcome to this deep relaxation meditation. In this session, we will be working toward relaxing both the body and mind.

Let us begin by going to a distraction-free place and getting into a comfortable position. You can either sit or lie down and place your arms and legs however you want. You will be here for quite some time so it is important that you remain as comfortable as possible. Relaxation cannot be achieved without comfort, after all.

Once you are ready, you don't have to close your eyes yet. Just follow my voice and take a deep breath now.

Excellent. Again.

In… And out…
In… And out…
In… And out…

Excellent. Now, continue to breathe for another while. You can let your mind and eyes wander as they please for now. Just continue to breathe normally and allow the mind and body to sink deeper into the state of relaxation. During this time, if you feel the need to close your eyes, you may go ahead and close them.

(Pause 1mn)

If you haven't done so already, go ahead and close your eyes now. As your vision fades to black, shift your focus to your own breathing. Take another deep breath through the nose, and out through the mouth.

Now, let us work on soothing the pain in your body. To do this, simply shift your focus to the top of your head and gradually move your focus down to the rest of your body.

Starting with the forehead now. Loosen the muscles in that area... Allow them to lengthen and relax... Let your eyebrows settle into their natural position. You might be squeezing your eyes. Allow them to relax.

Surrender to this tranquil darkness that surrounds. Surrender to the universe around you and know that you will be well taken care of.

Moving slowly down now. Allow your tongue to rest in its natural position. Allow your jaw to loosen. Allow all muscles of your head to soften, unwind, and relax.

There is nothing you need to do right now but to breathe and relax...

Moving down to your torso now... Relax those shoulders... Feel your arms becoming limp... Feel your fingers unfurling or curling up into their natural positions. Feel your arms loosening up... Feel your stomach moving up as you inhale, and down as you exhale. Feel the air entering and exiting your body as you breathe... Relax your entire torso...

Moving further down now to your legs... Again... No need to tense up any areas... Just let those muscles relax and unwind. Breathe deeply and allow that air to just wash away all the tension in your body... Feel your legs becoming soft and heavy, fully relaxed in the present moment.

Now, scan through your body again and notice any areas that are either tense or uncomfortable. We will now work on relaxing those areas as well.

Imagine that the air has the healing property that your body and mind need. Imagine that it is a golden healing aura. On your next breath, picture this glowing aura flowing into your body, infusing its healing energy to rejuvenate the body. Feel your body glowing softly as it soaks up all that positive energy. Allow your body to take whatever it needs to repair itself.

You have been working hard, you know? You might not have taken nearly enough care of yourself. Even so, you recognize the importance of self-care and self-love. You might be too busy in the past that you did not give yourself enough love or care.

But the fact that you are here, giving your body and mind the time and space they need to relax, is a sign that you indeed cherish the body that you are given. It is a sign that you do love yourself and that you are treating yourself the way you treat a loved one. That is what is called self-love – treating yourself like someone you love and care for. This love alone is so valuable that nothing even comes close to it.

The fact that you are taking care of yourself now is a gift, from you to yourself. It is a very beautiful gift. So, smile now in gratitude to yourself for you chose to take care of yourself. You choose to take care of your needs first so that you could function at your best.

If, at any point during this session, your mind starts to wander, simply remain with your thoughts for a few seconds. But do not linger for too long as some thoughts may provoke certain emotions and it will not do to get caught in those emotions right now.

There is a time and place for everything. Now is not the time to be worried, scared, anxious, or angry. Now is the time for the mind and body to relax.

As you continue to breathe and bathe in this beautiful healing aura, use the power of your focus to direct that energy and guide it to areas where you feel tense or pain. Allow your breathing to wash away all the pain and tension from your body. Allow the healing aura to go to that area, to repair, to rejuvenate, to heal those wounded areas, so that you may sink deeper and deeper into relaxation.

As we come to the close of this meditation, take another deep breath and count slowly down from 10. As I do so, feel your consciousness returning to your body.

10… Slowly coming back…

9…

8… Feel your consciousness returning to your body…

7…

6… Slowly wiggle your toes and fingers…

5…

4… Take a deep breath now…

3… Once more…

2… Coming back now…

1… You have returned.

Thank you.

Adult Bedtime Story 1 (60mns)

Thomas is startled as he awakens abruptly. He had nearly dozed off, his head having fallen backward to rest on the wall behind him. Thomas looks around and notices that he is not the only one.

All around him, early morning workers are catching a few more moments of sleep before arriving at their destinations, though no one else seems to have awoken at that moment.

"Must be one of those hypnotic jerks," he thinks, "Perhaps I hadn't even fallen asleep at all."

Thomas's daily commute is a particularly long one. He lives in his own flat at the southernmost end of the Northern Line in London. Despite the lengthy journey into work each morning, he never misses an opportunity to remind himself of how grateful he is to find an open seat. He is always one of the first on the train.

Perhaps he thinks the distance is worth the seated journey and Thomas think about the place he is whizzing off to at the early hour in the day. Thomas is a program manager for a small but well-respected software development company based in London. He has worked there for nearly eight years, having started there when he first finished his studies.

He enjoys the company of the people he works with and has a good working relationship with his boss but something in Thomas's gut contracts each time he thinks about walking into the office.

He watches this reaction come and then watches it leave though never forgetting that something is not sitting right. He arrives at work that morning and says hello to the others who have also arrived at 7:00 a.m. He prefers to get his day started as soon as possible so that he can finish up early and enjoy the late day sun as it falls upon the lush green parks of London.

His fingers get to work, typing away to clients, and working on projects. Sometimes, when the afternoon rolls around and the others have not yet returned from lunch, he takes a break from software to do some research on places he might like to visit.

Maybe Japan Australia or Greece. But on this particular morning, he is focused he's busy working on a new project for a startup company based in Athens. As he types away, his boss gently interrupts him with a proposal.

"Thomas I've been thinking," she says, "I had really loved for us to get to know the team in Athens on a personal level. I'd like to send you over there to meet our clients and to put a face to our name. There really is potential here for a long and strong relationship the first time in a long time."

Thomas beams and his heart flutters, a smile stretched from ear to ear. His boss, Louisa, takes this as a yes.

He'll spend five days in the city with plenty of time for both work and a bit of exploration. Thomas's mother is Greek, having grown up just outside of Athens. Many months ago, she moved to England when she was quite young returning only a few times.

Since then, Thomas himself has never been but has always felt a strong yearning in his bones to return to the place of his ancestors. Life has simply gotten too busy. He knows that this is no excuse and later that night, Thomas begins packing with glee.

Though he is not due to leave until the end of the week, Thomas struggles to contain his excitement, and understandably so. He calls his mother and father to tell them about his business trip. They were very delighted.

Thomas rests in his bed that night, looking out his window to the stars and the sky. The moon is nearly full, illuminating the city and the surrounding lands below. Planes pass by as flashing lights that effortlessly float across the universe.

Thomas thought to himself that he will soon be on such a magical vessel. He has not flown since he was a teenager and he is now approaching 30. Memories begin creeping into his mind. He thinks about his childhood and the strong bond he had with his grandparents.

His grandfather on his father's side was a farmer. Thomas remembers running through the fields with him and sometimes into the forest to collect wild berries and herbs. He always felt as if he was in a fairy tale when they wandered off into the woods.

Something about it felt mystical. Perhaps it was the way the wind would rustle the leaves or the sounds of the fluttering birds. Perhaps it was the crunching or tweaks underfoot. He loved the smell of evergreens and the way the light trickled in through the dense canopy overhead.

Perhaps he thinks it was a blend of all these things. Thomas remembers vividly the way his mother cooked, the way she laughed. The incredibly kind and loving mother he always knew and loved. Thomas remembers that he and his sister, Katrina, would help in the kitchen wherever they could. The two of them would rinse and dry the leafy greens and herbs and then help their grandmother cook the pasta sauce. They would stir, and stir, and stir as she added all sorts of aromatic herbs to the simmering tomatoes. Maybe that was how he was such a great cook today.

It has been a long time since Thomas had cooked. This realization stirred something in his belly. He missed it. He missed the slowness of time that enveloped him when he helped his grandmother prepare dinner.

It's been too long far too long. He thinks at this moment. Thomas vows to get back into the kitchen after returning from his trip to Athens. The week passes slowly until finally, Friday arrives.

With his bags packed, Thomas takes one last look around his apartment. He knows he's only gone for an extra-long weekend, but says "so long" anyways. While on the train to the airport, Thomas admires the greenery of London's outskirts.

The sun is shining and the May blossoms are a sure sign that spring has arrived. He feels quiet anticipation whirling in his heart. The trip is primarily for business, but he will have the entire weekend to explore the city of Athens before meeting his client on Monday.

It has been a long time since he has taken a trip like this and one to his mother's homeland is stirring his sense of adventure. His flight to Athens from London is only a few hours long. The plane soars through the clouds. Thomas looks down on the continent below appearing and disappearing as the plane moves in and out of the skies.

Thomas thinks how miraculous it is that humans are able to fly. As a child, he often dreamt about being able to fly. One particular reoccurring dream, he would watch himself sprout wings and soar across open fields and oceans.

He'd been awake, thinking that perhaps the dream was a prophecy for his future. Thomas laughs to himself at the recognition of this memory and thinks perhaps this sort of flying is not quite the same. Even so, it is certainly close enough.

The plane lands by early afternoon and Thomas makes his way into the center of town. He's staying at a small guesthouse within a short walking distance of the city's ancient ruins. He checks in and wanders up the spiral stone staircase to the third floor.

His room is immaculate with a delicate blend of rustic and modern touches. It is simple but it is all he could need. He takes a deep breath in and releases a sigh as he breathes out a wave of peace and comfort overcomes him.

A small balcony with sheer curtains covering the glass door that opens to the outside world. Thomas makes his way to the balcony and steps out his room looks out into the ancient acropolis. Athens buzzes below, a city ready to explore.

Thomas wanders through the narrow streets and alleys through markets and along winding roads that are lined with trees. With no map he feels entirely lost and yet, with no concerns in the world, he is taking the unknown road, allowing it to unfold as he goes step by step.

He takes a few set of stairs and wanders along cobblestone pathways until he reaches the foot of the Acropolis, staring up at this ancient fortress Thomas feels for a moment as if he is wandered back in time.

He wonders what it would have been like to live in ancient Greece. Countless myths come to mind as he recalls some of the stories his grandmother used to tell. He remembers feeling so very otherworldly, like the way being at the foot of the Acropolis feels to him now.

He pays his admission and ventures in, finding his breath having gone missing for just a few moments as he enters. Something has taken him aback, nearly moving him to tears. He surrenders to this space and to the emotion arising in him.

He realizes how long it has been since he allowed himself the trip to Athens. Thomas sees a version of himself that he can't quite describe but one that brings about feelings of peace, confidence, and clarity.

He breathes in and out effortlessly as he wanders the ancient Greek city. He dedicates the entire weekend to simply indulging in local cuisine, breathing in the history of ancient ruins, and sleeping soundly for as long as his body calls for.

All worries melt away as he grants himself permission to be entirely present with the land whose history courses through his veins. It has been a long time since he has slept so well.

He drifts off easily and awakes, feeling inspired and energized as he explores. He somehow forgets all about his meeting on Monday morning. But still, when the morning arrives, he packs his computer and heads to the startup small office in the center of town.

Thomas meets with Sam, the company's founder, and is introduced to the team he's been working with virtually over the past month. They talk about all things tech for what feels like hours.

Meanwhile, Thomas's heart is elsewhere. The meeting wraps up and Sam thanks him greatly for coming all the way to Athens to see what the company is like on the ground level. Thomas smiles and thanks him in return and heads back to his hotel for the final evening.

A mixture of emotions brews inside of him but he struggles to put his finger on what his heart is calling for on his final night in the city. Thomas sits on his balcony overlooking the ruins and the rest of the city.

The air is warm and the sky is clear, not a cloud covers the sky. The moon now waxing still casts a strong glow across the Earth's surface below. Thomas gazes up at it, feeling a vaguely familiar connection to the stars and the moon many years ago.

Thomas recalls being by the sea with his parents and his sister. Each summer, they would pack up the car and drive to a small bed-and-breakfast in the southwest tip of England. The days during these long summer weekends were slow, time was spent walking along the beach or wandering nearby towns and villages.

Evenings were early but Thomas remembers that on some warm nights, his father would prepare hot chocolate and fill a couple of cups to the brim. The family would sit beneath the stars, pointing out the few constellations they knew, at the same time sipping the sweet summer treat out of their travel mugs.

Now, Thomas feels nostalgia washing over him. Nostalgia for the days when he had fewer worries and was more connected to the natural world around him. He stares up at the moon now, feeling a wave of peace and comfort come over him as if it were a lullaby.

The moon overtakes him, offering a sense that it is now time to rest his body. It is now time to let his body sleep for the night. Thomas makes his way to his bed and dozes off swiftly and soundly.

Thomas returns to London the next day. Over the next few days, he feels a strong longing for something though he's not quite sure for what. He has a clear sense that it has something to do with his trip to Athens.

He misses the way that adventure made him feel it was as though a part of him was coming up to the surface, coming back to his conscious awareness senses that something is calling for his attention, but he's not quite sure what to make of it or what exactly it is saying.

Thomas struggles to focus on his work over the coming weeks. The voice is growing but he's starting to fear it. He wonders if it would have been easier had he never gone to Athens at all. He knows that something in him now is questioning the life he is living, but it feels too frightening to listen more closely to that voice.

It appears he has no choice. The whispers become louder and louder until finally becoming clear and confident. It told them with confidence that he should return to the roots.

He's not quite sure where the path will lead him though he knows one thing for certain. He must leave his job and return to the place that inspired him. He must return to the country that changed things.

Fear brews in his belly. He is not one for taking risks, preferring to take pathways that are safe and well-lit. He knows that he needs to jump. He knows that now is the time to take a risk. His future self, whoever that may be, is depending on it.

Thomas resigns, spending the next two weeks tying up loose ends and passing projects on to other team members. He prepares himself for the unknown. He thinks back to a quote by Lord Byron that he first heard some time ago. It reads:

"There is pleasure in the pathless woods by divine grace."

His sister returns to London from the United States to take over his apartment while he ventures back to the land their ancestors come from, unsure of where he is going. Thomas closes his eyes and places his finger on a map of Greece islands included to decide which road to take.

It lands on a faraway island in the Aegean Sea, on the small remote island. He books flights to reach this unknown land and packs his bags. Though he is not sure how long he will be gone for, he knows it will be at least a few months.

He's ready to reset entirely, not quite knowing what that means. He finds a small guesthouse online offering long-term accommodation and books for two months to start. It located high up in the mountains, in a small village, and with plenty of gardens around the property. It sounds just like what he's looking for

The plane lands a few days later in the south end of the island. Thomas calls a taxi that takes him to a small guesthouse in the tiny village of Menendez, a small town that overlooks the stretch of sea between Greece and Turkey. The owners of the small apartment he is renting lived just next door and come out to greet him they welcome him with open arms, showing him around the grounds that will be his home for the next few months.

They extend an offer for him to join them at dinner. Thomas unpacks his belongings and stares out the window that overlooks the surrounding mountains and the port below in the fresh mountain air.

He cracks open the window. he's not quite sure what he is doing here he knows he's in the right place. Thomas heads for the hills, packing a small bag with water and fruit to sustain him for the afternoon's adventure.

He walks through the mountains admiring the vastness of this small island. Low-lying shrubs blanket the land as red yellow and magenta blossoms brighten the primal landscape. The sun beams down from overhead as he walks, allowing his instinct to guide him.

He wanders the land with no plan, and no goal to guide him. He realizes it's been years since he'd walked this aimlessly perhaps not since childhood. He feels free, completely untethered, and prepared to begin again.

He had expected to be overcome with jitters during these first few days, but he feels quite at peace. Instead, occasionally, worried thoughts overcome his mind, hounding him with questions about what his plan is and what his intentions are. Though he knows that he does not hold the answers to these questions just yet, he reminds himself that that is okay.

Upon his return to the apartment, he witnesses how tired his body feels. He finds Maria and George, the owners of the guest house, and politely asks if he might join them the following night for dinner instead as he's feeling tired from the day's activity. They tell him to rest well and let him know that he is welcome to join them anytime.

Thomas slips quietly into bed and falls swiftly into a deep, deep sleep. That night, he dreams that he is an astronaut, floating far away in outer space looking down at the world and realizing how small it really is from way out in the galaxy. The earth feels like a very small home.

He realizes it is just one planet amongst millions of other floating bodies in the universe. This dream brings him a sense of wonder, inspiration, and a newfound appreciation for the earth he lives on and for the life that courses through his body.

From way up here, he can see that the earth is a home amongst other homes, and in the dream, he thinks, "Wow what a beautiful home I ended up living in."

Thomas awakens the next morning, feeling the clarity of the dream still with him, and in honor of the earth, he decides to walk yet again. He connects with the earth through each step he takes.

Somehow, Thomas feels as if he is a baby learning to walk for the first time. He's never given much thought to the ground beneath his feet but now he feels deeply connected to the land that supports him.

After some time, he reaches a secluded beach where he nestles himself into the warm sand. He revels at the way the sand seems to wrap itself around his body as he nestles in. Staring out at the ocean, he is reminded of the dream and of how the Earth revolves around as one complete unit.

In his bones, he now knows that he and everything around him lives and breathes together as a single organism. He breathes in the ocean air, feeling more and more settled in.

That afternoon, Thomas returns to the guesthouse feeling more energized and connected to himself and to the land. He makes his way to the second building on the property, to the home occupied by Maria and George, getting ready for dinner by chopping herbs, rolling small pieces of pasta, and preparing their home-baked bread.

He watches how intuitively their hands work with the food they are preparing and offers to help.

"I won't be as quick as you," he warns them, to which they reply, "Speed is not a desirable factor in our kitchen. If anything, we like when things move slowly,"

Thomas's reminded me of how things moved in his grandmother's kitchen and feels right at home. Over the next few days, Maria and George teach Thomas how to prepare local delicacies using herbs and produce from the land.

Along the way, it dawns on him. He has lost himself entirely to the kitchen, lost to the state of flow. His hands begin to work with the food and he prepares more effortlessly and intuitively.

Thomas is reminded of how much joy real food brings him. One night during his first week, he has another vivid dream. This time, however, he is in an open meadow. Beneath a large awning, wooden tables are lined up beneath the canopy and are adorned with lace tablecloths and freshly picked flowers.

Small twinkling lights lined the edges of the awning as dusk falls. His loved ones make their way to the table. Thomas stands at the head of the table and passes down dish after dish of food he has prepared for his friends and family. The group feasts, laughing and whispering beneath the midsummer night sky, savoring the head chef's succulent creations.

In the morning he awakes, knowing exactly what he is here for. He thinks about the voice that came to him just a few weeks ago that whispered, "Get back to the roots," and suddenly it becomes clear.

The roots he was meant to rediscover were not only the roots that connected him to Greece, but also those that permeate the land. He wants to know the earth through food. He wants to nourish the earth and the people on it through preparing wholesome plant foods and living in connection to the land.

He finds Maria that morning and joins her in the garden as he roams the rows of plants. He feels inspired to learn about each one, to get to know the way they grow. He asks Maria if she might teach him everything she knows and she beams. She would be honored to pass on her knowledge of the land.

Thomas remains on this little yet vibrant island for six more months, soaking up every bit of wisdom he can get. His heart and soul poured on to take care of the soil, to harvest, to forage, to cook.

When his final month in Greece comes around, he feels prepared to bring his knowledge back to his more permanent home of London and to begin his life again. Thomas's last morning in Greece, he wakes early in heads to his favorite trail through the mountains. The Sun has not yet risen and there are no signs of the world being awake just yet.

Thomas walks until finally, he reaches a small cave that looks over the sea. He nestles himself in as he watches the sunrise from the horizon. Thomas thanks the land for bringing him home.

He's grateful for having returned to Greece, but more importantly, perhaps he is blessed for having returned to himself. He thanks whatever higher-self within him helped him to take the unknown leap, but he would soon come to know that would change his life forever.

His flight takes off late that afternoon and he knows that he will one day return to this magical land and now he looks into the future, feeling ready to follow wherever it leads. Upon his return, Thomas spends a few months living with his parents in their country home.

Luckily his sister is happy to continue living in his apartment, offering him the time he needs to figure out what step to take next. In the meantime, he cooks, and cooks, and cooks until the refrigerator is empty of produce and stocked with savory plant-based meals.

He offers his mother two of her favorite traditional Greek foods he perfected. She is overjoyed by the delicious food he has prepared and by his rediscovered sense of purpose and inspiration.

Thomas enrolls in a culinary program upon returning home and soon after launches his own catering company. He focuses on bringing plants to plates in a way that feeds the souls of all nourishing both humans and the earth as one deeply integrated organism.

He starts off modestly, catering small events for his friends and family. Soon, however, his catering company blooms, touching the plates and palates of countless people across his country.

On the night after his first successful event, an event that brought city dwellers to the countryside for a feast beneath the stars, he dreams of another dream. This time, he rests on a beach on a faraway Greek island, looking out over the sea and thinking about how vast the ocean is he feels inspired and connected to both himself and to the world around him, sinking into the sand and listening to the waves rolled gently into and away from the shore.

It appears that nothing and everything happens in this dream, a feeling that has been with him since he first embarked on his Greek adventure many months ago. For the rest of his life, Thomas would often look back on his early days, thanking the unknown road for carrying him back to the roots. Each day he feels grateful for that first trip to Athens for it was that trip that changed everything.

Sleep Hypnosis for Deep Sleep and Relaxation (60mns)

Hello and welcome to this guided sleep hypnosis for deep sleep and relaxation. To begin, simply get into a comfortable position. It is recommended that you lie down in your bed and place your arms and legs however you want so long as it is comfortable for you. You will be here for quite a while and so comfort is of utmost importance. Without it, you will not be able to achieve deep relaxation.

At the end of this session, you will feel thoroughly relaxed and we can send you right off to sleep after this. So take a deep breath now to signal the body. To tell it that it is time to unwind, relax, and prepare for a night of restful sleep.

If you haven't already, go ahead and close your eyes. As your vision fades to black, shift your focus to your own breathing. Using your stomach, calmly breathe in and let the air flows in, filling your lungs entirely. Use your diaphragm to breathe, so that your lungs can be filled with air.

Focus on your breathing and use it to anchor yourself in the present moment. Just before you exhale, feel that gentle stillness in your body. Focus on how it feels. Observe every breath that you take and notice how relaxed your body becomes at each breath.

As you balance your awareness between the past and the future, there is a space. In this space between the past and the future is a freedom, a power, a silence, as you observe it, you notice its beauty.

It is calm. It is everything

If you observe your mind returning to the past or imagining the future, gently guide your focus back to the present. Be present in the present moment, allowing the observation of the breath to keep you present and centered. Allow yourself to relax at every exhale.

With the eyes closed, imagine standing on a beach on a beautiful spring day. To accommodate the gentle slope of the sand toward the water, you lean ever so slightly to the soothing and consistent tumble of the water's edge onto the shore as its timidly approaching and withdrawing as the small waves find their end.

Observe the tiny ripples over the surface of the water as the wind calmly travels on its way. You notice a subtle salty scent in the crisp fresh air, feeling happy and content. A gentle smile spreads on your face. This is a special place just for you this is your place.

Happy and content standing on the beach as you look out beyond the reef, you notice the distant hum at the same time as silent splashing of large waves colliding with the enormous rocks beyond the bay's calm water.

Looking back on the beach, you notice the resilient and lush plant life that leans onto the edge of the beach and toward the shore as best it can. Noticing the beautiful blue sky, you see a bird glide still as if floating on the breeze.

That same breeze gently cools the skin from the warmth of the sun. Scanning the surrounding further, you see that some leaves and foliage gently sway in the wind while others are perfectly still with surprising pockets of colorful wildflowers spread throughout the landscape.

At the end of the beach, you see the hues of grey and bronze on the surface of rocks. Rocks that have shared the beach with the wind, the water, and the sand for thousands of years, creating shapes beyond artistic imagination, creating an almost symbiotic relationship between nature's elements.

Feeling the sand underfoot, firm yet shaping to mold the base of the feet in this beautiful place, you feel so calm and relaxed. You see a beach chair sitting in the sand. Take yourself to that chair and rest comfortably.

In front of you now appears a large screen and, on that screen, you see all the things you do using energy to stay awake, every conceivable measure to prevent sleep see them all now on that screen.

Now if you sleep and rest thoroughly you will have an oversupply of energy. What would you really like to do with that energy? What constructive or instructive or developmental project would you like to undertake to use up that extra daily allotment of energy?

You've got to direct it elsewhere rather than keeping yourself awake. That nice rest each night is going to replenish your energy. how are you going to use it? As you contemplate this, you are projecting your thoughts onto the screen in front of you, allow these thoughts to roll like a movie reel as you watch on the screen all the things you would really like to do with that energy how are you going to use it

As those thoughts play on the screen in front of you, begin to elevate out of the body, leaving behind the thinking part of you in that beach chair to watch its thoughts without you as you drift away floating up, feeling free and liberated, distancing from your thoughts, feeling light and free as you float freely.

Within your mind, imagine a soft black velvet couch that has a warm and comfortable feel about it. It sits a large and wide. One end of the couch is shaped like a bed as you stretch out on the smooth soft velvet which feels ever so nice.

It creates within you a comfortable drowsy feeling. You take a deep relaxing breath as that feeling becomes more and more comforting, and all-encompassing as you drift off into the realms of sleep as thoughts into your mind allow these to drift across the soft black velvet and disappear off the edge then return to resting calmly and comfortably.

The sound of my voice just like a lullaby lets you sleep deeply and soundly feeling calm feeling safe and feeling relaxed. Distanced from your thoughts you rest and sleep easy knowing that all shall be well and now is the time for sleep.

Treating yourself to a night of deep and restful sleep. All shall be well. Each time you listen to this, you drift deeper and deeper into a calm and restful sleep easily and naturally sleeping deeply recovering and replenishing the mind and the body.

Sleep now, feeling relaxed and at peace. Sleep now calmly and deeply. All shall be well as thoughts into your mind allow the east to drift across the soft black velvet and disappear off the edge then return to resting calmly and comfortably in your mind as though these words are your own.

"As I sleep easily, I am filled with positive energy I sleep restfully and deeply as like leaves falling from a tree I let go of thoughts and worries allowing them to drop away. As I sleep freely and easily I am free from the past and the future all shall be well."

"I am filled with gratitude and peace as I sleep easily and peacefully, I am caring for myself and accepting the love within me. As I sleep deeply and restfully, I take care of my mind and body I sleep easily and at will, I sleep restfully and deeply. All shall be well."

Distanced from your thoughts you rest and sleep easy knowing that all shall be well and now is the time for sleep.

Treating yourself to a night of deep and restful sleep. All shall be well. Each time you listen to this, you drift deeper and deeper into a calm and restful sleep easily and naturally sleeping deeply recovering and replenishing the mind and the body.

Sleep now, feeling relaxed and at peace. Sleep now calmly and deeply. All shall be well as thoughts into your mind allow the east to drift across the soft black velvet and disappear off the edge then return to resting calmly and comfortably in your mind as though these words are your own.

"As I sleep easily, I am filled with positive energy I sleep restfully and deeply as like leaves falling from a tree I let go of thoughts and worries allowing them to drop away. As I sleep freely and easily I am free from the past and the future all shall be well."

"I am filled with gratitude and peace as I sleep easily and peacefully, I am caring for myself and accepting the love within me. As I sleep deeply and restfully, I take care of my mind and body I sleep easily and at will, I sleep restfully and deeply All shall be well."

Distanced from your thoughts you rest and sleep easy knowing that all shall be well and now is the time for sleep.

Treating yourself to a night of deep and restful sleep. All shall be well. Each time you listen to this, you drift deeper and deeper into a calm and restful sleep easily and naturally sleeping deeply recovering and replenishing the mind and the body.

Sleep now, feeling relaxed and at peace. Sleep now calmly and deeply. All shall be well as thoughts into your mind allow the east to drift across the soft black velvet and disappear off the edge then return to resting calmly and comfortably in your mind as though these words are your own.

"As I sleep easily, I am filled with positive energy I sleep restfully and deeply as like leaves falling from a tree I let go of thoughts and worries allowing them to drop away. As I sleep freely and easily, I am free from the past and the future all shall be well."

"I am filled with gratitude and peace as I sleep easily and peacefully, I am caring for myself and accepting the love within me. As I sleep deeply and restfully, I take care of my mind and body I sleep easily and at will, I sleep restfully and deeply All shall be well."

Each time you listen to this, you drift deeper and deeper into a calm and restful sleep easily and naturally, sleeping deeply recovering and replenishing the mind and the body sleep now feeling relaxed and at peace.

Sleep now.
Calmly and deeply. All shall be well.

As thoughts into your mind allow these to drift across the soft black velvet and disappear off the edge then return to resting calmly and comfortably in your mind as though these words are your own.

"As I sleep easily, I am filled with positive energy I sleep restfully and deeply as like leaves falling from a tree I let go of thoughts and worries allowing them to drop away. As I sleep freely and easily I am free from the past and the future all shall be well."

"I am filled with gratitude and peace as I sleep easily and peacefully, I am caring for myself and accepting the love within me. As I sleep deeply and restfully, I take care of my mind and body I sleep easily and at will, I sleep restfully and deeply. All shall be well."

Distanced from your thoughts, you rest and sleep easily, knowing that all shall be well, and now is the time for sleep, treating yourself to a night of deep and restful sleep. All shall be well.

Each time you listen to this, you drift deeper and deeper into a calm and restful sleep easily and naturally sleeping deeply recovering and replenishing the mind and the body sleep now feeling relaxed and at peace.

Sleep now.

Calmly and deeply. All shall be well.

As thoughts into your mind allow these to drift across the soft black velvet and disappear off the edge, then return to resting calmly and comfortably in your mind as though these words are your own.

"As I sleep easily, I am filled with positive energy I sleep restfully and deeply as like leaves falling from a tree I let go of thoughts and worries allowing them to drop away. As I sleep freely and easily, I am free from the past and the future all shall be well."

"I am filled with gratitude and peace as I sleep easily and peacefully, I am caring for myself and accepting the love within me. As I sleep deeply and restfully, I take care of my mind and body I sleep easily and at will, I sleep restfully and deeply. All shall be well."

Before Sleep Hypnosis for Relaxation (60mns)

Hello and welcome to this before sleep hypnosis for relaxation. In this session, we will be working toward relaxing the body and mind so that you can achieve a night of restful sleep. It is important that you have such a night of sleep as it provides you with the maximum energy and you will wake up the next day feeling fresh and ready to start the day.

So, without further ado, let's get started. Begin by getting into a comfortable position on your bed. It is recommended that you lie down and place your arms and legs however you like so long as you are comfortable. Comfort is of utmost importance, after all. If at any point during this session, you feel uncomfortable, you may move around gently to ease that discomfort.

Take a deep breath now to signal to the mind and body that it is time to unwind and relax. Allow yourself to bring your full awareness to your own complete comfort. If you haven't already, go ahead and close your eyes and shift your focus to your breathing as your vision fades to black.

This sleep hypnosis experience is all about letting go of your previous day. This trance experience will help you to let go of your past day's activities and any of your day's leftover thoughts and all of that day.

The time now spent energy just like soft echoes, disappearing in the distance as you comfortably and serenely falling into sleep. Now, imagine as best you can, effortlessly and completely releasing yourself from all of that daytime's physical stored tension as it also gives yourself the intention to release your mind's tensions.

Releasing from all of those weightier concerns by making a conscious choice to turn down all types of conscious thoughts and to turn down that more tiring, heavier, mental chatter.

They, just like you in these moments now, are choosing to move into all calming bedtime peace receiving the good news and the great news to further relax the conscious thinking mind.

And it's really a comforting and reassuring reason to pause all of those thoughts because there's really so very little here for the thinking mind to do, except to settle you back and to stretch you out more comfortably a little more and more.

Because even now, you're more comfortable, allowing yourself to let go and rest back, allowing yourself to become more in tune as your deeper ears continue to listen, allowing all of these powerful familiar sweeping automatic processes to proceed and unfold now as if all by themselves.

You know you're allowing your sleeping relaxation so swiftly and so speedily to slow all of those thoughts all the way down. You are resting your entire body now, feel every muscle lengthening and softening, becoming more and more relaxed as all parts of you, physically and mentally, increasingly relax, enjoying your whole, your body slowly unwinding and uncoiling, moving away from those old tensions.

And all of your own inner encouragement just remains as a peaceful reminder that you are in fact so safe and so in control of this session because you understand that really are all ready to descend even deeper and deeper into this blissful hypnosis.

Simply choosing to relax with all of those beautiful intentions to just easily sink you and relax you all of the ways down, as more and more parts of you are growing and unfolding you into your most powerful, peaceful, a blissful journey of sleep.

You're realizing you're moving so tranquil into those loveliest levels of the mind and your body feels entirely at peace. This arrival and this unfolding of your peace and your total relaxation only arrive as fast as you know. You can wish it as you choose to take in some slower and deeper and even more relaxing breaths.

These resting parts of you are realizing you're beginning to imagine in ways so much more because it's so pleasing for these parts of you - now just wander about as you wander and dream and let yourself dream of how deeply your deepest of all relaxations.

All of these relaxing sensations now progress inside of you even more, always unfolding you into calm within this space of your trancing mind. This full awareness allowing all of these calming resources to take you there.

It may be that very soon, there is some noticeable sense or feelings of even more serenity, moving you forward and yet simultaneously moving you deeper down, just moving you and traveling you in these relaxing beautiful ways as all of your trancing comforts becomes the relief of a day well spent.

And passing now as those echoes travel through you and into some unique and curious passages which will ease you through these states of peace and tranquility. It's the conscious mind back there that was holding so tightly onto all of that business and those more active thoughts.

As this freedom from conscious thought takes you more and more freely as you begin to float away, all of those ideas of wakefulness are really now dissolving so well and just evaporating.

At this moment, you know that everything is okay and that all will be well. It is very natural for all of those less conscious thoughts to also unfold as you move here and there and observe every passing thought like clouds drifting across the sky.

These thoughts also carry your awareness to wherever and whenever that may now be because so many more blissful and peaceful sensory inputs of that tranquility those calmest sensations really do begin to rock you so gently. Every passing second you spend here is another step further into relaxation.

And somehow these tingles of serenity and these vibrations of the bliss filling you so softly and gently with all new satisfactions and the joys of this deeper essence of pure asleep, arriving because your unconscious mind does remain aware of these words as it feels so safe to rest in these ways.

Focusing now so gently to be so easily open and receive all of these important messages of your growing calm. As you're aware of some even more subtle undercurrent and frequency of peace and serene transmissions just like restful delta waves of pure healing feeling inside of you with lasting elixir years of absolute peace.

Because all of these sounds and these words and these meanings you know are purely positive inspirations for your most restful self and all of these tunes are in ways are so frequently becoming so familiar and as welcoming to your total rest.

It was always encouraging you so gently to your total confidence, to really connect you, and help you and motivate you to get a real handle on those pillars and those foundations of relaxation.

As these very real foundations of your total calm are expanding and broadening your comforting self out every breath you take as you inhale slowly now is changing you with rejuvenation and every breath you braid out is transforming you with an even deeper bliss.

As this evolving yet simple process of your natural breathing continues all by itself, constantly releasing you from all tensions and all negativities and sometimes it's just as easy as that to imagine one by one or even all at once your subconscious enjoyment constantly delivering you with such a union of bliss into all of these natural ways into your most tranquil calm, as this deep flow is deeply unchaining you and unshackling you from everything unwanted.

All of those muscles are loosening and you feel all of those nerves and their fibers giving up their once held unwanted strains because relaxation now is quickly wrapping all around you and passing over and even into you just like a beautiful cloak of pure energy that melts away all the constrictions and opens your heart each and every time.

You now enjoy falling just like this into your absolute deepest of all deep sleep, because you're sleeping self is enjoying all of these entrancing kinds of states. You're always moving with your perfect natural resting pose and your own perfect tonics just like potions of inner health swirling and calming inside you.

As you move into your restful composure, these sensations pass down within you so easily and smoothly just like a soothing aromatic scent as your senses fill with that serenity. You can feel this relaxing aura flowing from the very top of your head, flowing down gently and ever so slowly, yet so soothing and relaxing and therapeutic, flowing just like honey, all the way down to the tip of your toes, covering you with a relaxing aura. You feel at ease, safe, relaxed, yet powerful, and confident at the same time.

And you're deliberately sending and receiving the sleeping health with such a beautiful and softly glowing beam of imagined white light just like a candle of constancy and blissful awareness, shining its protections all over you and penetrating each loosening muscle, throughout every lengthening joint, as these deeper words are reaching you.

You feel yourself growing softer and smoother inside like so many older leftover worries or concerns are disappearing, fading into thin air, leaving no trace behind, as if they are never there.

You are aware of your entire tangible essence, which is now receiving so much more beautiful relaxing aura into every cell because your inner core is now rejuvenating, and the essence of your vital being is beginning to quickly wind back because your inner glow of youthfulness and your vitality is now rebuilding and restoring and positively changing you inside in so many ways

As you reset your body's energetic clock and just like imagining those clocks hands moving backward, you're allowing all types of new and restorative health to repair you with these sensations in these visions with so much more health and healing restoring you and your youthful outlooks as you unlock this total rest.

So smoothly and efficiently. It's effortless. You feel yourself grow constantly here, and yet never a day older. You feel so much younger in this deeper mind as you gently enjoy rebalancing your inner happiness you are aware on some much, much deeper levels of your deepest self, so easily allowing you and opening you to release all of those special chemicals of sleep.

So many of those wonderfully felt natural endorphins of sleep are in pure health, because the more you do relax in this way and continue to enjoy all of these sounds and all of these healing healthy words, you feel you're sleeping more and more just like a baby sleep.

You feel that soothing caresses and sleeps frequencies and tones transform with pure repair, as the rest of that is already here, imagining so many subtle massaging softest waves bringing so many welcoming tingles of your flowing energy.

Your beautiful sleep continues to work, curate, and lengthen you as you continue to relax through all of this stretching moments because, in this slowing time of slumber, you're allowing all durations of your timely sleep to be so full and natural and extended to precisely the length of your very best duration of perfect rest.

As so many good feelings and wonderful feelings of satisfying, gratifying, sustained relief continue to carry you onwards and always deeper, with all of your days past energy now disappeared.

All of those days, past activities, you're saying, "So long, long gone". All of that old busyness is now completely spent as all of those long fading moments of those distant sunshine hours.

Now, all of these instead fade away into the mind as the mind rests. They fade into the distance just like the sunset on the horizon. You feel yourself gliding all the way down, slowly yet surely, deeper into relaxation, gently falling as a floating leaf.

Down, and down, down to meet your landing as you land into spacious peace. These lovely peaceful parts of you are landing and touching down so softly floating further onto a feathery pillow of absolute rest, or just like that floating ways as you see it move down to be gently carried away upon the loveliest the most caring bubbling types of crystal streams.

As all of these warming flowing waters unwind you inside and wash you, they relieve you of even more weight and you're breathing again with a sigh of deepest relief because you're unloading all of that worry, stress, or tension that may have been across your shoulders as you watch that floating leaf simply traveling and bobbing as it flows along those deepest rivers where you're observing all streams and their currents carrying away all leftover worry so far away.

As you continue to float so safely, you're moving out into that perfect source and arriving in this time to these soothing happiest dreams as you see yourself becoming so aligned and feel so light.

Here, we're coming just like light rays, becoming white, full of purity and perfection, transforming and changing you with such delight as twilight's deepest comforts continue to flow within you.

This peace always continues transforming you as you clear yourself and release more and more easily, removing any past concerns because you're releasing everything unwanted and just taking all of that away letting go of everything that is no longer required.

As you send those energies so far, far away and these inner sensations and these visions are now turning you because your most serene sensors are now beginning to ascend you, with the wings of your perfect calm sleeps, floating soaring and uplifting, or at least is now carrying your piece by piece. You're moving higher and higher within such parts of you becoming so free to fly out above.

And you're moving directly into all of your healthiest happiest enjoyable dreams now, throughout all of these infinite spaces of sleep's perfect ideals because you're ascending and becoming the very essence of this freedom, becoming just as those white rays now, moving you into that beyond all solar systems and or galaxies.

Your sleep is expanding beyond all of those heavens as you now see and imagine yourself just like a shining shooting star. You're moving with this clearest crystal light as if the lightness of the universe calls you to move even further beyond.

You're now moving into your sacred dream's space, feeling, and knowing that you will remain here because you're traveling through all the heavens. Your sleeping form is so sublime. You're so safe and protected here in your total rest and now allowing yourself to more deep sleep.

As all parts of your sleeping self are resetting you to your divine perfection, you're becoming once again just like one with this universe, so stunningly free and cleansed and released from all past energies.

Throughout all of your sleep, henceforth, you will rest more peacefully because you know that you will sleep so well after having experienced the magic if your deepest and best sleeping self.

You can sleep to your full and healthiest duration each and every time you choose to sleep and your bedtimes, you can easily and effortlessly fall fast asleep anytime you choose just as soon as your head touches that pillow or as soon as you decide to completely rest yourself down.

All of those thoughts and all aspects of your thinking mind are simply resting and all parts of your body are simply calming down. They know how to relax and they will send you into sleep immediately and instantaneously.

As you breathe deeply once again, and so calmly, so easily, imagine yourself lacing yourself into your total sleep because you are remaining here right now as you re-energized your deeper self and restoring your deeper self in all of these magical and positive ways as your inner being and your outer being remain so fast asleep, sleeping so well.

So, my lasting wish for you as your rest remains so pure is that you do easily and effortlessly sleep on and rest so deeply. Even as my voice and these words begin to fade, you know you continue to feel wonderfully good and positive each and every time you fall into your sleep.

Just as these moments right now, you're sleeping, and until we talk again, I wish you the very best. May you enjoy your most relaxing and pure sense of calm. May your restful sense of perfect continue as you sink deeper and deeper into sleep, and my voice becomes faint because you are resting and relaxing as you remain so deeply asleep.

Thank you and goodnight.

Guided Mindfulness Meditations & Bedtime Stories for Busy Adults: Beginners Meditation Scripts & Stories For Deep Sleep, Insomnia, Stress-Relief, Anxiety, Relaxation& Depression

By Meditation Made Effortless

Table of Contents

DAY 1—LEARNING TO BE CALM [5 MINUTES] 1

DAY 2—BREATHING INTO RELAXATION [5 MINUTES] 2

DAY 3—WINDING DOWN THE DAY [5 MINUTES] 3

DAY 4—LUNCHTIME RELAXATION MEDITATION [10 MINUTES] 4

DAY 5—MORNING MOOD BOOSTER MEDITATION [10 MINUTES] 6

DAY 6—QUICK ANXIETY REDUCING RELAXATION [10 MINUTES] 8

DAY 7—10 MINUTE PANIC ATTACK RELAXATION [10 MINUTES] 10

DAY 8—DEEP RELAXATION [15 MINUTES] 12

DAY 9—SUNSET MINDFULNESS [15 MINUTES] 14

DAY 10—AFTER WORK STRESS-RELIEVING MEDITATION [15 MINUTES] 16

DAY 11—PAUSING FOR RELAXATION [15 MINUTES] 18

DAY 12—THE ALERTNESS MEDITATION [15 MINUTES] 20

DAY 13—CALMING AFTER A PANIC ATTACK [15 MINUTES] 22

DAY 14—EASY-TO-FOLLOW SELF-HEALING MEDITATION [20 MINUTES] 24

DAY 15—SELF-CONFIDENCE MEDITATION [20 MINUTES] 27

DAY 16—THANKFULNESS AFTER A FULL DAY [20 MINUTES] 30

DAY 17—DEALING WITH HEAVY EMOTIONS [20 MINUTES] 33

DAY 18—THE DARKNESS AND INTO NOTHINGNESS [20 MINUTES] 36

DAY 19—FLOATING ON WATER [20 MINUTES] 39

DAY 20—THE CANDLE MEDITATION EXERCISE [25 MINUTES] 42

DAY 21—GUIDED MEDITATION FOR DEEP SLEEP [30 MINUTES] 45

DAY 22—SELF-HEALING MEDITATION [30 MINUTES] 48

DAY 23—STRESS RELIEF MEDITATION: LOOKING AT THE STARS [30 MINUTES] 52

DAY 24—BEFORE SLEEP DEEP RELAXATION MEDITATION: REFLECTING ON YOUR JOURNEY [30 MINUTES] 55

DAY 25—RELAXED MINDFUL EATING: GUIDED MINDFULNESS TO APPRECIATE YOUR MEAL BETTER [30 MINUTES] 59

DAY 26—MORNING ANXIETY-REDUCING MEDITATION TO KICK-START YOUR DAY [30 MINUTES] 62

DAY 27—GUIDED MEDITATION FOR REDUCING ANXIETY: LISTENING TO THE WIND [30 MINUTES] 66

DAY 28—STRESS-RELIEVING GUIDED MEDITATION—OVERCOMING CHRONIC FATIGUE [30 MINUTES] 69

DAY 29—STARING AT THE MONSTER & FACING THE ANXIETIES WITHIN: GUIDED MEDITATION TO OVERCOME ANXIETY [30 MINUTES] 73

DAY 30—GUIDED SLEEP MEDITATION: OFF TO LA-LA LAND… [40 MINUTES] 77

DAY 1—LEARNING TO BE CALM [5 MINUTES]

Welcome to your first day of guided mindfulness meditations. This book is perfect for busy people who are always on the go. This book aims to give guidance to each individual who looks for mindfulness and relaxation in their lives. By picking up this book, you are marching your way to a more mindful existence. You can look forward to relieving your stress, decreasing anxiety, and just feeling light.

For the very step of your journey, all you need to do is to learn how to calm yourself. That's about it. It seems as simple as it sounds, but it' actually very challenging. That's why you will be introduced to some key concepts that will help you with your mindfulness journey.

The first concept is to be 'in the here and now'.

What does this mean?

"Am I not in the here and now already?" you may be asking yourself.

Well, if you are beset with so many thoughts, if something is bothering you, if you seem to be unaware of what's happening in you and around you, then you are not in the here and now… Your body might be in the present… But your mind might be somewhere else… In the past, or somewhere far ahead in the future…

That is why you need to stop… Pause…

Close your eyes… Try to channel in the feeling of relaxation, of calm…

Then take a deep breath… As you do, try to block everything out… Just pause…

Maintain the deep breathing… Concentrate on it…

Think of your breathing as the only thing that matters now…

Take another deep breath…

Think of the words 'here' and 'now'….

Be in the here and now… And take in relaxation as you draw another breath…

Now… be in a state of calm…

DAY 2—BREATHING INTO RELAXATION [5 MINUTES]

As you learned the first key concept on day one, day two will introduce you to the technique that will greatly enhance your day one experience. Concentrating on your breathing is crucial to attaining relaxation. This will help you prime your mind so that you can achieve being in the 'here' and 'now' much faster.

Try to find a comfortable spot where you can have a few moments by yourself. Claim this spot as your own. You need your alone time to refocus, relax, decompress, and practice mindfulness. Settle into this spot and position your body in such a way that it will relaxed and calm. You may close your eyes as you do this exercise.

Take in a long and deep breath…

Breathe in… Hold… And then release…

Be very intentional as you draw and release your breath… Try to imagine the air going inside your nostrils and into your throat and windpipe… And finally, imagine the air settling inside your lungs… There it circulates for a few seconds… And then visualize it making its return voyage back to the outside…

Try to block out errant thoughts that may enter… Concentrate on visualizing your breathing… If thoughts do enter, then just let them be… Quickly acknowledge their presence and then let them pass… Continue visualizing your breath…

Breathe in… Hold… And then release…

Bring in relaxation as you inhale…

Breathe in… Hold… And then release…

Feel the calmness as oxygen fills your lungs…

Breathe in… Hold… And then release…

Relish at the calmness and peace you have achieved as you expel your breath…

Maintain the rhythm of your breathing… Continue to visualize the air that enters and leaves your body…

Be in the here and now…

And when you are ready to end your exercise, you may open your eyes…

DAY 3—WINDING DOWN THE DAY [5 MINUTES]

It's always great to have an opportunity to wind things down as the day comes to a close. After a hectic day, it's important to slow things down a bit. You will gain a deeper appreciation of your day if you take a few moments to reflect on it as it ends. This exercise will teach you how to slow down. It will let you revert the hyper-speed pace of life back down to normal speed. This is important as you gain a better understanding of yourself and of the world around you.

To begin, go back to your comfortable spot. The best time to do this is during sunset or as your workday is about to end. Go to your quiet spot to be alone. Make sure that this spot is free from your usual distractions. Try to disconnect from the outside world for a few moments, so turn off your mobile phone.

Start to take in a very deep breath… And close your eyes…

Breathe in… Hold… And then release…

Again, imagine the air that enters your body… See it in your mind's eye as it enters your body, penetrating each cell… See your breath bring you life-energy… And then see it flow out of you… bringing with it the cares and worries that you accumulated throughout the day…

Breathe in… Hold… And then release…

Breathe in… Hold… And then release…

Be in the here and now… In the here and now, time moves a little slower… You were running on hyper-speed earlier in the day… And that was needed for you to achieve your goals… Now that kind of rush is no longer needed… The workday is done… You don't need to run in fast-forward…

Go with the flow of time now… The pace is much slower… Your body is now still… It is getting more relaxed as it arrives in the here and now… Let your mind decelerate… Hit the brakes a little bit… Take it slow now…

Take it slow… Wind things down…

Let relaxation and calmness flow through you… This is what you need… This is what your body needs… And this is what your mind needs now…

Wind things down… Because the day is winding down as well… Time to get back to normal speed…

Breathe in… Hold… And then release…

As you get back to normal speed, feel free to make light movements. Feel and appreciate life at an unhurried pace… And then open your eyes…

DAY 4—LUNCHTIME RELAXATION MEDITATION [10 MINUTES]

This quick lunchtime relaxation meditation will offer you a respite that will bring your energies up as you tackle the second half of the day. It is important to be mindful of your energy level as the day progresses. There might be some mornings where, even though it's still early, your energies are already depleted. This exercise will help you replenish your energy as you go through your lunch break.

For this exercise, you need to find a place where you can be alone. Make sure that this place is somewhere free from distractions. It is best to go through this exercise away from other people so that you won't be bothered. So settle yourself and get comfortable so that you can begin.

Close your eyes… Try to release the tensions you are currently feeling…

You are on a break… This is the time where you can re-energize yourself… This is a time for you to pause… These few moments where you can achieve some form of rest from your break is crucial to your success later in the day…

Take in a long and deep breath…

Breathe in… Hold… And then release…

Visualize the air that you take in… Imagine it enter and leave your body… Visualize the air giving you a sense of lightness… It is making you feel more relaxed… Let the wonderful air flow inside of you… And then outside of you… In and out… In and out…

Breathe in… Hold… And then release…

You can feel your head feel light… Your neck and shoulders feel the same way too… It's like some burden is lifted off of it…

Your muscles are starting to relax as well… You can feel them slowly giving in to the lightness… This wonderful feeling energizes you… It reinvigorates your spirit…

Breathe in… Hold… And then release…

Be in the here and now… This is your time… This is the time for you to rest and recuperate… Maximize this time given to you…

Breathe in… Hold… And then release…

Good energy is starting to surround you… Let it ease away all tensions… Let it soften the tightness that you feel… Experience the good energy… And let all the negative energies flow out of you…

Breathe in… Hold… And then release…

You are in the here and now… In the here and now, the past and the future do not matter… In the here and now, you can recharge… Let your breathing recharge you… Feel the oxygen being distributed throughout your body… Feel your inner energies surge… Let this slow burn give you the energy you need for later…

Concentrate on your breathing… Concentrate on letting the good energy flow… This is how to be in the here and now…

Breathe in… Hold… And then release…

It's time to end your lunchtime relaxation meditation… It's time to face the day once again… Feel the surge of energy in your muscles. Do light movements, wiggle your fingers and toes, and then shake your arms and legs… This will let the energy flow through you. And then open your eyes. You are ready to face the rest of the day…

DAY 5—MORNING MOOD BOOSTER MEDITATION [10 MINUTES]

Mornings are the perfect time of day to boost your energy level. A great start to your day will usually ensure that you will finish your day strong. What's great about the morning is that you can have time for yourself to be alone, especially if you do this exercise really early. This mood booster will really help keep your energy levels high all throughout the day for superior performance.

For this exercise, it's advisable if you wake up early to do this. Go to your sweet spot from day one. Get comfortable. You can do this while still in your pajamas or sleepwear.

Let the stillness of the early morning bring you relaxation as you settle in to your comfortable position. And when you're ready to begin, close your eyes.

Start by concentrating on your breathing…

Breathe in… Hold… And then release…

Feel the freshness of the early morning air… Feel its vigor as it tries to wake you up… The air you breathe is full of energy… It is doing its best to energize each cell inside of you…

Visualize the air surrounding you… Try to see their form in your mind's eye… See the presence of this air and the energy it brings…Then imagine it entering your body as you inhale… And also imagine it going out of you as you exhale…

Breathe in… Hold… And then release…

Be intentional in your breathing… Focus on imagining your breath… Be as detailed as you can be… This is the only thing that matters now… In the early morning, it's just you and your breath….

Breathe in… Hold… And then release…

Be in the here and now… You are here where you find yourself… You are in your comfortable quiet place… And the now is the early morning… You took the time to be in your quiet place…

This thought brings you stillness and calmness… The here and now relaxes you… Because you know that the past and the future don't matter in the here and now… There will be another time and place for them… But not in the here and now…

In the here and now, it's just you and your breathing… That's what matters in the here and now… In the early morning, you are alone with your breath…

Breathe in… Hold… And then release…

Feel the rise in energy that is concurrently happening as the sun is starting its ascent… This is the power of the early morning… Feel the coolness of the air as it swirls around you… This is the coolness that the early morning gives… Notice the absence of noise… This is the kind of peace and quiet that the early morning offers…

This is the here and now that you find yourself in… Take it all in… Appreciate it… Let the early morning give you life… Let it give you the energy you will be needing for the day…

Breathe in… Hold… And then release…

It's time for you to start your day. Allow the morning to continue to bring you relaxation and energy. You can open your eyes when you're ready. And then get up—you should feel the energy flow through you now. Let this energy power you to success.

DAY 6—QUICK ANXIETY REDUCING RELAXATION [10 MINUTES]

Your anxieties come to you every so often without any announcement. They spring their attack suddenly and you are often caught by surprise. Sometimes, these anxieties are just there as you go through your day. They accumulate and build up until you can no longer take it and they start to spill over. That's why it's best to take some time to practice mindfulness and meditation in order to reduce you anxieties. This exercise will hopefully do just that.

You may do this exercise anytime you feel your anxieties starting to build up. You never know when you will have an anxiety attack. It's best to prevent these attacks by doing this exercise. Find a quiet and private space where you can be alone. Settle into a comfortable position and close your eyes.

The key to reducing anxiety is the notion of stopping. You need to stop. You need to pause. You need to cease whatever it was you were doing, whatever it was you were thinking… Just stop…. Pause…

As you close your eyes, try to become aware of the sensations that are trying to flood your senses… You might feel some weight on your head and shoulders… Your muscles might also be tensed… And there could also be butterflies in your stomach… Don't worry, these are all natural reactions to anxiety… This is your body telling you that it is experiencing anxiety just as your mind is experiencing it…

It is important to bring in awareness and focus on your breathing….

Breathe in… Hold… And then release…

Again, visualize your breath… Imagine the air as it enters your nostrils… Imagine the full details of this thought… Be very intentional in your breathing… Desire each breath… Really take time to feel it… Continue imagining your breath as it now reaches your lungs… See in your mind's eye your lungs enlarging with the presence of air… And then see your lungs distribute this oxygen to every cell in your body… And then it's time for this air to go out… Continue to imagine your lungs, this time it is contracting as it liberates itself from the air… And then imagine this air exiting from your nostrils as it rejoins the outside world…

Be very intentional in your breathing… Desire every breath… Know that this is the only thing that matters in the here and now… Because you are in the here and now…

Breathe in… Hold… And then release….

You are in the here and now… And in the here and now, your anxieties are far away….

Know that in the here and now, the past is no longer relevant… In the here and now, the future does not yet matter… Your anxieties are residents in the past and in the future… Therefore, they are either no longer relevant, or they still do not matter…

In the here and now, It's just you… and your breathing… In the here and now, you are calm… In the here and now, you are reclaiming lost energy… This was the energy you lost worrying over the past and the future… Reclaim all that energy you lost… It is yours for the taking, right here and right now…

Breathe in… Hold… And then release…

It's time to bring yourself back… Feel your body respond to the renewed energy… Slowly bring your senses back by making slow and measured movements… And once you're ready, open your eyes and get up. You will find yourself re-energized. You should also have renewed focus and your anxieties will have been greatly reduced.

DAY 7—10 MINUTE PANIC ATTACK RELAXATION [10 MINUTES]

You were on to a great start yesterday by learning how to reduce your anxieties. For this day, you will learn how to respond whenever you experience a panic attack. Sometimes, you will not be aware that you are already in the throes of a panic attack. What started out as a simple moment of fear might suddenly morph itself into a full blown panic attack. Panic attacks will cause you to freeze up. You will be debilitated by it. And it may be to your detriment because you will not know what to do. This exercise will hopefully free you from the clutches of panic.

This exercise can be done anytime and anywhere. After all, you cannot time panic attacks. So when you find yourself panicking, then you can activate this exercise.

Again, start by gaining awareness of yourself and the situation. If you find yourself overcome by great fear and this fear is starting to get in the way of you acting on it, then that could already be a panic attack. It is best to pause at this point. Stop what you are doing. Try to also stop whatever it is you were thinking. This is difficult to do, especially when you're already panicking. You can achieve this by concentrating on your breathing.

Concentrate on your breathing now…

Breathe in… Hold… And then release…

Be intentional… Be deliberate… You can ward off all those thoughts if you can build more awareness into your breathing…

Breathe in… Hold… And then release…

As you inhale, count one to four… As you do, picture out the numbers… Do the same when you hold your breath and when you exhale…

Breathe in… 1-2-3-4

Hold… 1-2-3-4

And then release… 1-2-3-4

Do it again… This time try to slow down your counting a bit…

Breathe in… 1… 2… 3… 4…

Hold… 1… 2… 3… 4…

And then release… 1… 2… 3… 4…

Be intentional in your breathing… Be intentional in trying to slow it down… Count the numbers and picture out each digit in your mind as you do so… Do your best to try and slow down the counting… This will slow down your breathing… In turn, it will also slow down your heartbeat…

Breathe in… 1… 2… 3… 4…

Hold… 1… 2… 3… 4…

And then release… 1… 2… 3… 4…

Now feel your heart's pace slowing down… As you concentrated on your breathing, it allowed your heart to slow things down… And with your heart beating at a more measured pace, it has also allowed your mind to decompress…

Breathe in… 1… 2… 3… 4…

Hold… 1… 2… 3… 4…

And then release… 1… 2… 3… 4…

Feel the panic start to subside… It starts to dissipate as your mind starts to regain its control… Your mind is also sending out a message to the rest of your body… Your mind tells your body that it is back in control…

Now feel the tensions you earlier felt ease up a bit. Feel some of the burden that weighed you down earlier lift… The fear is still there but the panic is gone…

The best thing you can realize at this point is that you are back in control… Panic is no longer holding you down… It does not bind you… It has released its grasp… You are free to take control… Take back the control…

Breathe in… 1… 2… 3… 4…

Hold… 1… 2… 3… 4…

And then release… 1… 2… 3… 4…

All it takes is to take back control of your breathing… This is how you fight back the panic attack… This is how you gain back control of yourself… All you have to do is to be in the here and now… Panic cannot touch you in the here and now… In the here and now, you can move, you can take action… you are in control…

Breathe in… 1… 2… 3… 4…

Hold… 1… 2… 3… 4…

And then release… 1… 2… 3… 4…

Now open your eyes and do what you have to do… You are now back in control…

DAY 8—DEEP RELAXATION [15 MINUTES]

Today marks the second week of your guided meditation for mindfulness journey. Congratulations for committing seven straight days of practicing mindfulness. The exercise today will focus on bringing you deep relaxation. This type of relaxation is perfect to end a busy day. The great thing about this exercise is that the duration is not that long. In fact, deep relaxation can be achieved in just 15 minutes.

To start, go back to your sweet spot. You should have established for yourself a place or venue where you can do your mindfulness exercises. Go to this place and settle in—start to feel comfortable. You may change into more comfortable clothing as this may help you breathe better.

Dim the lights and close the door and the windows. You want to ensure peace and quiet for this exercise. Close your eyes as you become more comfortable in your position. And then you can begin.

Start by focusing on your breath…

Breathe in… Hold… And then release…

Imagine the air that you are breathing… Try your best to imagine the air… Like it is visible… And you can see it enter your nose… You can see it fill your lungs… You can also see it exit out of you… Focus your thoughts on this and this alone… Relegate your other thoughts… Bring these unnecessary thoughts to the background… On the foreground of your mind is the air that you breathe…

Breathe in… Hold… And then release…

Be in the here and now… Let your cares and worries drift away… They leave you knowing that they don't matter in the here and now…

Breathe in… Hold… And then release…

Picture out your whole body… Try to imagine the whole of your present in your mind's eye… See your body as it is now… How are you now? How does your body feel?

As you gain awareness of your body, try to imagine your breath bring in relaxation to it… Every breath you take allows you to absorb relaxation… It settles inside of you as it disperses all throughout your body… And then as you exhale, all your cares and worries go with it… The tension and tightness that you felt a while ago are starting to also disappear…

Now feel your muscles relax… They become soft, like putty… Slowly but surely you are drifting into a more relaxed state… You can sense the lightness overcome you… Now you feel like you are floating on air… weightless… Nothing is holding you down… You feel delighted as you take in the experience…

And now your head is feeling light as well… You can feel all the cares and worries start to drift away… These errant thoughts are being replaced by thoughts of calmness and peace… of relaxation and stillness… of lightness… of weightlessness… of delight and bliss…

Breathe in… Hold… And then release…

Appreciate the feeling of deep relaxation… This is how it feels to be relaxed… This is how it feels to when your cares and worries are nowhere to be found… This is how it feels to be in the here and now…

Take another long and deep breath… Continue to be very intentional in your breathing… Bring in great desire as you execute each of your breaths…

Breathe in… Hold… And then release…

As you continue your breathing with great desire, realize that as your mind and body relax, your spirit relaxes as well… Imagine a light that glows within you… It has grown dim as it burned most of its energy trying to combat your tiredness and anxieties… But imagine this light now… It glows just a little brighter… It shines brighter as you breathe in and breathe out…

This is your soul… And it is recharging… As your body and mind relax, your soul is also regenerating… Continue with your breathing… Let the rhythm of your breathing increase the energy of your light within… Feel your body respond… Your body is getting more and more relaxed…

Remain in the here and now… It's time to bring yourself back… Bring in another burst of air…

Breathe in… Hold… And then release…

You have just undergone a relaxation experience so deep… You are refreshed… Bring awareness back to your body… Make slow movements to signal your intent to come back… And then you can open your eyes… Take another deep breath and then you can continue with your day… May you enjoy the remainder of your day and have a good night's sleep later…

DAY 9—SUNSET MINDFULNESS [15 MINUTES]

The sunset has a restorative and healing power. You can certainly feel its effects and power if you take the time to see and experience its beauty. Let the power of the sunset bring you closer to mindfulness with this exercise. All this exercise requires from you is for you to sit back, relax, and enjoy the beauty of the sun as it calls it day.

You need to be outdoors for this exercise. Try to find a nice and quiet spot outside. Make sure this place is devoid of people—you want to enjoy only your own presence for this exercise. So settle down in this place and get comfortable. There will be no need to close your eyes for this exercise. You need them opened so that you will be able to enjoy the full majesty of the sunset. Time your exercise as the sun is about to set. This should take about fifteen minutes so make sure you can be at your spot fifteen minutes before the sun sets.

Start by bringing your awareness to your breathing…

Breathe in… Hold… And then release…

Breathe in the late afternoon air… Let it introduce calmness within you… The day is about to end… There's no more need to rush… Life is starting to slow its pace once again… Let your mind and body move at the world's current pace… It is back to normal speed… It is back in the here and now…

Be in the here and now… And in this afternoon you find yourself perched on your sweet spot ready to take in the majesty and brilliance of the sun as it sets…

Be in the here and now… Just like the sun… The sun is always in the here and now… In the here and now, the sun understands its place, understands about the passing of time… Its place is as steady as it has always been… Its time is ever constant, ever running… Know that it is us who move… We are forever in motion… And it seems to us that it is the sun that is moving… But it's an illusion…

The sun has always been in the here and now… It stays in place and always acknowledges the time… We need to be in the same place and time as the sun… To be in the here and now…

Breathe in… Hold… And then release…

Our now is the experiencing of the sunset… It is one of nature's gifts to mankind… It is as constant as time… It is forever there, because as long as the sun rises in the east, it will surely set in the west… That is the message of the sun to us… And it is up to us to behold its beauty and wisdom…

For the sun is in the here and now… We, too, can be in the here and now… Just like the sun…

Behold the sun as is slowly moves down… down to the horizon… Behold the soft hues and the gentle light that the sunset brings… Notice the beauty of everything the light touches… The light of the sunset brings out the soft colors of the world around you… Appreciate the softness… Appreciate the beauty… This is the sun's gift to you…

Breathe in... Hold... And then release...

See the clouds in their striking colors... See the yellows, reds, and oranges... Notice the hints of blue fading... The fiery colors are invading the sky... Try to see if you can spot hints of purples and pinks on the sky... See the whole sky and all its beauty... The sky is like a painter's masterpiece... It is like a canvass that has been touched by the paintbrush of a master... This is the sun's gift to you...

Breathe in... Hold... And then release...

And so the sun settles on the horizon... It slowly descends until you can no longer see it... The sky is left radiating with the colors but it grows darker now... The sun has called it a day...

And you should also call it a day as well... It's time to wind down your activities... It's time for rest...

This is the here and now that you find yourself in... The here and now that calls for you to slow down and rest... Tomorrow will be another day full of activity... And you can be sure of that just as sure as the sun rises in the east...

Go on... Continue with the rest of your day at a slower pace... Rest and recharge... The sun has set...

DAY 10—AFTER WORK STRESS-RELIEVING MEDITATION [15 MINUTES]

So the workday is finally done and you can now start to kick back and relax. You had a full day and it was all about making sure you achieved your goals. For sure your day was full of physical and mental activities. These activities will take a toll on your mind and body. It is best to practice mindfulness and try to achieve some relaxation as you close out your day. This exercise is the perfect activity to gain that stress-relief as you end your busy day.

Make sure that all your tasks and activities are done before you start doing this exercise. Go to your sweet spot and settle in. You might want to have dinner first before doing this activity. And a warm shower will do you good as well. Once you're ready, settle down and get comfortable.

As always, bring your focus to your breathing…

Breathe in… Hold… And then release…

Start to get a sense of how your body is feeling right now… Feel the sensations of your body… Let these feelings manifest themselves…

Try to feel the tightness of some of your muscles… Can you identify these spots? What particular areas are feeling tight? These are probably the areas that did most of your activities… These must be the areas that brought you the success you achieved today… You can feel proud of these muscles… They served you well….

Next, try to feel the tiredness of your legs and feet… They brought you to places… They made sure you stood up… They held your weight… They are another reason for your success… Feel proud of your legs and feet… They served you well…

Now try to feel your back and shoulders… Maybe you can feel some aches and pains as you move… Your back has held you steady all throughout the day… Again, your back and shoulders are another reason why you got through your day just fine… You can feel proud of your back and shoulders… They served you well…

Lastly, feel your head… feel your mind… It must feel heavy after all the mental processing you did as you worked… Appreciate the power of your mind… This piece of bodily organ is making sure you are functioning well… And it brought you ideas and thoughts so crucial for your success… Feel proud of your mind… It served you well…

Breathe in… Hold… And then release…

Breathe in… Hold… And then release…

Breathe in… Hold… And then release…

Let your breathing bring forth relaxation… Let it bring you rest… Let it ease your overworked mind and overburdened body…

Each breath you take makes the tension that you are feeling go away… Your breathing is causing your muscles to relax… Imagine the air your take in reach your whole body… It untangles the knots in your muscles… It lets your muscles free… It lets them breathe…

Imagine also your head and mind feel freer with each breath that you take… Your breathing is freeing your mind from its worries… It also sweeps away the cobwebs and the dust that has started to accumulate in your mind… You can feel your head feel light…

Your back, shoulders, and neck also feel freer… They can respond much better to the movement now as you breathe in more relaxation… You can feel the tightness ease away with each breath you take…

Breathe in… Hold… And then release…

Remember that you are in the here and now… Your body is starting to rest in the here and now… Your body is starting to bring its energy back… Your body is recuperating…

And as you continue your slow and steady breathing, you can see stress escaping your body… Stress was the key component of your brilliant performance earlier in the day… You needed that stress in order for you to function at your peak…

But the day is about to end and all your activities are done… There's no need for the stress anymore… There's absolutely no need to hold on to them… So let them escape you… Maintain your breathing and continue to be in the here and now…

Breathe in… Hold… And then release…

In the here and now your stress is dissipating…

It's time to bring yourself back… Start by bringing more energy into your muscles… Start to move them slowly… And then open your eyes and stand up… You can get through the remainder of the day with your stress greatly reduced…

DAY 11—PAUSING FOR RELAXATION [15 MINUTES]

It's just nice to be able to pause sometimes. When the day gets too hectic, when life starts to move a little too fast, it is but appropriate to stop for a few moments. This will enable you to get your bearings back. You can reorient yourself and gain that little bit of extra energy needed for you to finish strong. This exercise will enable you to activate this pause. And hopefully, it will bring you the relaxation your need.

As you gain awareness that your day might be headed for a frantic finish, it's important to just stop… Just pause… Hold off whatever it was you were doing… Just stop and try to regain your balance…

Try to find a place where you can be alone… It would be hard to pause and meditate if there are so many people with you and around you… So go to this place… Excuse yourself… Tell the people you're with that you need just fifteen minutes… This is all you need to be able to pause and relax… And then you can continue and get on with your day…

As you settle into your spot, try and get comfortable… You might be feeling heavy sensations… You could be going through some anxieties… Don't worry, these things are normal… Feel free to acknowledge these feelings and anxieties… But do not dwell on them… Try to let them pass as you acknowledge them… Let them be on their way… You need to be able to relax first…

Get a hold of yourself and bring your focus to your breathing…

Breathe in… Hold… And then release…

Breathe in… Hold… And then release…

Breathe in… Hold… And then release…

Let your breathing slow down your body's motions… Let it slow down your heartbeat… As you gain more control in your breathing, you will find your heart rate start to slow down… You need this sensation so that you can feel that you are back in control…

And with this control back, bring yourself to the only place and time you need to be… In the here and now…

It is in the here and now that you can pause… It is in the here and now where you can stop and take stock of what's happening… It is in the here and now where you can let your mind and body rest for a little bit…

Breathe in… Hold… And then release…

In the here and now time starts to move a little slower… It moves in consonance with your heart… It moves to the rhythm of your beating heart… The more you slow your breathing down, the more it seems like time is creeping and crawling at a snail's pace…

Let this feeling bring your relaxation... Let it bring your calmness... This relaxation and calmness are what your body and mind need right now... Let the relaxation and calmness relieve you of your burdens, even if the relief is only temporary...

Breathe in... Hold... And then release...

Just be in the here and now... The here and now is you not doing anything... The here and now is what allows you to just stop... The absence of activity allows your mind to be at ease... It allows your mind to regroup...

By pausing you are bringing your control back... Stopping has allowed you to reclaim this control... You handed this control over to your cares and worries momentarily... But you retrieved it... You pried it from their clutches... Because they do not own control... You own it... You are in control...

So control whatever it is you can... And for those that you can't, let it go... Those are not in the here and now... What is in the here and now are the things that you can control...

Breathe in... Hold... And then release...

Now it's time to restart... You had your time to pause... You regained possession of your control... You can continue with your day... Your pause will enable you to finish your day strong...Take a deep breath and count backward...

Breathe in... 3...

Hold... 2...

And then release... 1...

Open your eyes and continue with your day...

DAY 12—THE ALERTNESS MEDITATION [15 MINUTES]

Wouldn't it be great to have a burst of alertness when you start to feel lethargic and listless? Well, it is possible. You can get a dose of alertness just by focusing your mind. Mindfulness can elevate your energy levels and bring you to a state of alertness. All it takes is for you to make time and a private place and you can be on your way to alertness. Try this exercise to bring out the alertness in you.

Excuse yourself and find a place where you won't be bothered. As you feel the thralls of lethargy and boredom, you need time for yourself to bring your energy levels back. So go find a private space. Settle down and get comfortable. Begin the exercise once you feel settled…

You can close your eyes to help ward off distractions… Start by focusing on your breathing… Imagine the air that surrounds you… Try to envision visible air… It is all around you… It swirls, dances, and floats…

Now imagine yourself bringing that air inside your body as you breathe… You can see the air traipse and dance as it makes its way into your nose… And then visualize the path it is taking as it enters your body… See with your mind's eye how it travels from your nostrils to your airways to your lungs… And as it enters your lungs it gives it power and energy… This is the same energy that is distributed all throughout your body… And then picture how the air behaves as it leaves your body…

Breathe in… Hold… And then release…

Your body and brain have grown listless… It has grown tired… Perhaps it got overwhelmed by too much information… Perhaps there was nothing that created a spark… Perhaps it is just tired… You can feel your attention and focus starting to decline…

But notice how your body and mind behaves as you breathe… Notice how they react when oxygen is introduced to them… They actually gain more energy with each breath that you take… Your body and mind need air… It needs the energy brought by the oxygen…

So get a hold of yourself… And get a hold of your breathing…

Breathe in… Hold… And then release…

Breathe in… Hold… And then release…

Breathe in… Hold… And then release…

Bring yourself in the here and now… The here and now is the only place and time that matters… The here and now will bring you to alertness…

Breathe in… Hold… And then release…

You can start to feel a slight spark start to emerge from within you…

Breathe in… Hold… And then release…

The spark starts to intensify… Slowly at first…

Breathe in… Hold… And then release…

It now becomes a fire that burns… You can feel the heat… You can feel the energy…

Breathe in… Hold… And then release…

This fire that burns from within gets bigger and bigger with each breath you take… Let it burn brighter…

Breathe in… Hold… And then release…

This fire is your alertness… This fire is your energy… It is alive once again… Your breathing jumpstarted it… Let your breathing bring forth your desired energy… Feel it surge once more… Your energy will bring with it alertness… And permit this alertness to bring you vigor as you go through your day's remaining activities…

Continue to be in the here and now… Let your breathing rhythm continue… Each breath brings with it the oxygen needed to enable the fire that burns within you burn brighter…

Breathe in… Hold… And then release…

You have regained your alertness… You can now go back and finish what you need to do… You now have the energy necessary to get through the day… Feel your alertness continue to rise as you take in each breath…

And now you are ready to get back… Maintain your breathing rhythm as you bring yourself back… Feel the energy surge… Let your body adjust to your surroundings… Move them a bit so that you can start to bring yourself back… And when you're ready, open your eyes… You should now be able to get back to your day feeling recharged and full of alertness…

DAY 13—CALMING AFTER A PANIC ATTACK [15 MINUTES]

When a panic attack grips you, you will usually find yourself unable to move. You will feel that you are paralyzed even though your body is still able to function. What's happening is that your brain becomes so overworked by the panic it feels that it will have a hard time commanding your body. That is why it is important that you regain your control as fast as you can. And you can only achieve that once you feel calmer. This meditative exercise can help you achieve that calmness.

You can start this activity the moment your panic attack starts to subside. As you gain a little composure, you can then decide to pause. You need to stop your activities. If you can, you also need to put a pause to whatever it was you were thinking.

This pause can be achieved by putting focus on your breathing. So close your eyes and bring your awareness to your breathing…

Breathe in… Hold… And then release…

It will do you well to be mindful of how you breathe… Bring in intentness with every breath…. Be deliberate as you allow the air to enter your body… Do it with such a desire that it brings newfound energy to your body… Focus on it… Experience it… Live it… Be aware of your breathing…

Breathe in… Hold… And then release…

And now bring yourself in the here and now… Know that this is the only place that matters… The fears that you experienced earlier, the cause of your panic, well, they do not exist in the here and now… It's either their existence has come to pass… These are your fears that happened in the past… Or these fears have yet to happen… Once again, they do not matter… Not here… Not now…

Breathe in… Hold… And then release…

The here and now is about you taking back control… The here and now is you being deliberate in your breathing… This is your way to bring control back… You know that this will enable you to be closer in the here and now…

Now allow calm to enter your body… Allow calm to enter your mind…

You have put your fears in their place… You have transported them to somewhere not in the here and now… That place is where they belong… They shouldn't hold residence in the here and now…

You can actually let calmness in now with your fears in their proper place….

Feel the calmness start to infiltrate your body… They can now start to penetrate your core… This calmness takes away the messy feelings you were feeling when you started to panic… This calmness is taking away the weight that pinned you down earlier... Allow the calmness to work its magic... Allow the calmness to transport you to another place... A place where you are in control...

Breathe in... Hold... And then release...

You gain more calmness the more you breathe... Steady your breathing... Let it follow its natural rhythm...

Feel the calmness flow down to your lower body... Feel it take the pressure off your feet and legs... You feel more nimble now that your lower body is unburdened...

Feel the calmness settle in your core... It enters at the seat of your soul... It brings you the warmth you needed... The warmth you lost earlier when you were panicking... The calmness brings you a sense of security... It emboldens you... It takes some of the doubt away...

And then feel the calmness do its wonders on your mind... You can now think clearer thoughts... The fear that blocked your thoughts earlier is gone... It is now replaced by the calmness that you feel... Your mind feels sharp... You can now focus... You feel so in control... This feeling brings back the confidence you lost earlier... It boosts your ego... Now you know you can get through with this challenge just fine... Because you are calm...

Breathe in... Hold... And then release...

Appreciate the steadiness that you feel now... Know that you can gain control of yourself once you let the calmness in... You can gain control of yourself as you bring yourself in the here and now...

Remain in the here and now...

Breathe in... Hold... And then release...

And now, feel free to bring yourself back... The panic attack you felt a while ago is not here anymore... It is now replaced by calmness... It is now replaced by steadiness... Feel that you are in control of yourself by moving your body... Know that your body follows your mind's every command... No need to dwell on your fear... You have placed that fear where it belongs... You can now stand up to that fear... You are confident enough to face it... And when you're ready, open your eyes... Welcome back!

DAY 14—EASY-TO-FOLLOW SELF-HEALING MEDITATION [20 MINUTES]

Your mind is very powerful. It is powerful enough to heal itself. And it is more than capable of healing your body. All you need to do is to divert your focus and point it straight into your self-healing capacity. Tap the power of your mind so that it can do the process of convalescence. This meditation exercise is the clincher for your second week of practice. As such, you will continue by focusing on mindfulness as you try to achieve relaxation. But the ultimate goal for this exercise will be self-healing. And through this exercise, it can be done in an easy-to-follow method.

Start the exercise as you did in the other relaxation exercises—go to your comfortable place. Situate yourself in a position that will bring you relaxation and calmness. You can wear loose clothing so that your body can be well-ventilated and can breathe better. Dim the lights of your room and focus on intensifying your relaxation. You can start by closing your eyes.

As always, bring your attention to your breathing. Put in all your effort and attention to how you breathe… Let all your desire flow with the air that you take in… Be intentional as you go about it…. Be deliberate… Do it purposefully… Be one with it…

Breathe in… Hold… And then release…

Visualize the air that you breathe… See it in your mind's eye… Trace its journey from the outside of your body to the inside… Visualize how it travels from your nose to your lungs… Imagine the air reaching your core… Imagine it giving you life… Imagine it allowing your cells to burn energy… And then continue to trace its journey… This time as it makes its way out of you… Imagine the air sweeping with it all the impurities in your body along with it as it exits you…

You are breathing in relaxation and energy… You are expelling your body's impurities as you exhale… Let the goodness in… And let the tension and tightness out…

Breathe in… Hold… And then release…

Try to remember your goal… Try to remember how it is to be mindful… Just be in the here and now… The here and now is the only place and time you need to be in…

Be in the here and now as you focus on your breathing… Be in the here and now as you visualize taking more and more relaxation from the air around you… Be in the here and now as you imagine all the impurities being expelled from your body as you exhale…

Breathe in… Hold… And then release…

Breathe in… Hold… And then release…

Breathe in… Hold… And then release…

Now try to feel your whole body… Feel where it hurts… Feel your ailments… Feel the parts of your body that are not well… Go ahead and take your time… You are in no hurry… Just feel… Let the pain and discomfort reach you… Just feel these conditions that are in you…

And then feel the sensations that these pain and discomfort bring with them… What other feelings do they give you? Try to feel all of them… Put them together with the ailments… Let them take part in this exercise… Go ahead… Just feel them… Take your time…

Breathe in… Hold… And then release…

Breathe in… Hold… And then release…

Breathe in… Hold… And then release…

Remember that you are in the here and now… And in the here and now you feel some discomfort… You also feel pain… You feel some sort of sickness… Your head is heavy… Your body is languid… Your muscles feel tired… Your whole body is in disarray… Go ahead and feel these sensations… It's perfectly normal to feel these… These are the symptoms of an unwell body…

Now it's time for you to heal yourself…

Imagine a bright light shining on top of your head… This bright light starts out as a small ball at first… And then it grows bigger… And it gets brighter still… Its radiance intensifies… And you can now feel its warmth…

This is the healing light… This is the light that will enable your body to recover… This is the light that will ease all discomfort… This is the light that will try to take away the pain…

Let this light enter you… Allow its radiance to shine upon you… Starting from your head, down to your toes… Let the light cover you completely… Let its luminescence pierce through your skin… Give consent to it… And let it do its wonderful work on you… Let the healing light start your self-healing process…

Breathe in… Hold… And then release…

The power of the healing light makes you feel all warm inside… You feel a delightful sensation as it swathes your whole body with healing energy… You are starting to feel more relaxed… The light is bringing you to a whole new level of calmness… It makes you feel very comfortable… very still…

And pretty soon you start to notice your body responding to the healing energy of the light… You start to feel very light… Your muscles do not harbor the tightness it felt earlier… Your head is free from the burden that troubled it a while ago… Your whole body is glowing with the energy of the light… You are starting to heal… Feel the healing process… Feel the discomfort and pain start to subside…

Breathe in… Hold… And then release…

You are bringing in more relaxation as you breathe… And you are expelling pain and discomfort more and more…

And you are still in the here and now... In the here and now you are healing... Your body is regenerating... It is restoring itself... So that you can function better... So that you can have more freedom... So that you can live your life unhampered... So that you can stay longer in the here and now...

Let your thoughts remain with the light... It covers you with such brightness that you can feel a tingling vibration from within... This is the power of the healing light...

And then it's time for the light to go... It slowly leaves you... But the healing process continues... Stay with the feeling of healing...

Breathe in... Hold... And then release...

Reacquaint yourself with your surroundings... Try to move your body a bit... Stretch your muscles so that you can feel the energy recirculate... And then open your eyes... You have just undergone self-healing...

DAY 15—SELF-CONFIDENCE MEDITATION [20 MINUTES]

A lack of self-confidence can hamper your performance big time. Sometimes, doing well is just a matter of having the right levels of confidence. You can do great things if you believe in yourself. But confidence can prove to be elusive at times. What do you do if your supply of self-confidence seems to be in short supply? You can dig deep within you and let your mind manufacture it. That's right, you can will yourself to be more confident. And you can do it through a mindfulness meditation exercise.

For this exercise, you need to be in a place where you can be alone. This place should preferably have a mirror. It is best to do this exercise before you attempt at a pressure-packed performance. Or you can do this regularly as you retire for the night.

Start by facing yourself in the mirror. You may stand for this exercise. Standing will give your body more energy. And more energy means more confidence. But feel free to be seated if you wish. Look at your reflection straight in the eye…

And then you can start focusing on your breathing…

Breathe in… Hold… And then release…

Maintain eye contact with the person you see in the mirror while you breathe…

Notice the contours of the face of the person in the mirror… Try to see the shapes and forms that you can see before you… See the person in front of you reflect your every action… Bring the person you see in the mirror in the here and now…

Breathe in… Hold… And then release…

Remember that the only place and time that matters is the here and now… Doubt and regret have no place in the here and now… In the here and now, it's just you… Just you and the person you see in the mirror… That person is also you… And you can feed the person you see in the mirror with confidence…

Visualize the air around you… See with your mind's eye this air that surrounds every inch of the room you are in… Know that the air around you has energy… And this energy is what you need in order to bring in confidence within you…

You need to take in this energy in the air…

Breathe in…

Hold… Let the energy intensify as you hold your breath…

And as you release your breath, blow it to the person in the mirror… Let the person in the mirror receive the energy from your breath… This is the energy that will give the person you see in the mirror confidence… Observe your reflection doing the same… The person in the mirror is also blowing energized air to you… Receive this air… Receive the energy… Feel your confidence rise… Feel yourself soar higher as you take in more and more energy… You have received a much-needed boost in confidence…

Continue to blow the air to your reflection…

Breathe in… Hold… And then release…

Breathe in… Hold… And then release…

Breathe in… Hold… And then release…

Now say to yourself, "I am confident!"

Say, "I can overcome this. I know I can do this. I will do this… I'm doing this now."

Say, "I have what it takes to succeed."

Feel your energy rise as you say each word… Feel your confidence reach a higher level with each utterance…

And now it's time for you to visualize success… Visualize how your victory will look like… You may close your eyes for this… Play it out in your mind… Picture yourself executing and performing with great confidence… Picture yourself performing your best… Picture yourself at your peak… Let this picture stay with you… Let it be etched in your mind…

Be in the here and now… You are focusing on increasing your confidence… You are visualizing success and victory… You have put doubt and regret to the side where they cannot bother you… Because doubt and regret have no place in the here and now….

Breathe in… Hold… And then release…

Now it's time to open your eyes… Time to take a look at your reflection again… See the person in the mirror… And see the difference… Notice how the eyes of the person in the mirror sparkle with confidence… Notice the smile starting to form on the face… It's a smile of self-assurance… But this self-assurance does not border on overconfidence… It is just enough to lift the spirits of anyone who sees it…

Appreciate the spirit of the person you see in front of you… See the aura of the person in the mirror… It burns brighter… You can no longer sense doubt… All you can see and feel is confidence… Appreciate the beauty of the person in front of you… Appreciate how confidence can bring the best out of that person…

And then realize that the person you see in the mirror is you… The confidence that you can sense is the confidence that is inside of you… You upped your self-confidence as you heightened the energy you got from within…

Breathe in… Hold… And then release…

Now it's time to conclude this exercise… Take in another long and deep breath…

Breathe in… Inhale the energy that's in the air…

Hold... Let the energy intensify as you hold your breath...

And as you release your breath, blow it to the person in the mirror... Give your reflection energy one last time...

Take a good look at yourself and then move away from the mirror... Continue to feel your confidence soar... Feel the wonderful feeling of increasing your energy and your confidence... You may stand up... And as you do, continue to let your energy and confidence increase... Then go about the rest of your day with great confidence...

DAY 16—THANKFULNESS AFTER A FULL DAY [20 MINUTES]

Your day will end on a high note if you choose to cap it off in high spirits. A thankful heart will always lighten the mood. This thankfulness will enable you to see all the good that has happened within your day. This will allow you to see that the glass is indeed half full. So end your day with a thankfulness meditation. This exercise will teach you how to be aware and how to be mindful of all the good things that happened to you.

This exercise is one of the lighter exercises in this book, if not the lightest. You can do this anywhere. You can even do this while walking. All you need for this exercise is a time and place. That's all you need for you to be in the here and now…

Start with your breathing… Put your focus on it… Desire every breath you take… And then be forceful as you release that breath…

Breathe in… Hold… And then release…

Just go with the flow of your breathing… Follow its rhythm… Become aware of it… Let your breathing sing a happy duet with your heart beat…

Breathe in… Hold… And then release…

And as you release your exhalation, exclaim a silent "thank you"…

Feel the lightness of your heart as you do it… Feel your heart flutter as you utter the silent word of thanks… Feel your heart fill with gratitude… And let this gratitude bring in joy… Let it also bring you great satisfaction…

Once again…

Breathe in… Hold… And then release…

And don't forget to say another thank you… You can't utter thank you enough… Feel free to say it over and over again… In fact, say it again now… Say, "thank you"….

This is your heart speaking… This is your heart telling the world how much it appreciates being alive… How much it appreciates being able to take in the sweet air… And that's why you exclaim a thank you with each breath… Let each moment be a moment of joy… Be grateful for this… Be grateful for your existence… Let your existence remain in the here and now…

Think of all the wonderful things that happened today… Think of all the joyous occasions that transpired… Think of everything that made you smile… These are the things that made you enjoy your day… Be thankful that these occasions became part of your life today…

Now think of the not-so-happy happenings… Think of the hurt and the pain… Think of the ugly and the disastrous things that happened… Feel them weigh you down… But let them quickly pass… The reason why you're feeling them now is that you also want to be thankful for them… Be thankful because they are still a part of your life… Life is not worth living with these happenings… You take the good with the bad… For how can you appreciate the good things in life without the bad things? Be thankful still… These are the happenings that remind you that you're human after all…

Breathe in… Hold… And then release…

Breathe in… Hold… And then release…

And now think of the people that are close to you… These are the people that matter most to you… These are the people you care about… These are the people you love… Try to see each of their faces in your mind's eye… Let their image stay with you for a few moments… Try to feel their presence even if they're not there with you…

Go ahead, take your time in thinking about these people… After all, these are the people you love… These are your friends, colleagues, neighbors, family, children, partner, lover… These are the people that make you who you are… These people helped shape you… These people are also the reason why you continue to strive and do your best in this world…

Think of these people and say their names under your breath… Go ahead and name them one by one… And as you do so, say a word of thanks to them… Thank them for making your life the way it is… Thank them for making a huge impact on your life… Just thank them… For being there for you when you need them…

Breathe in… Hold… And then release…

Breathe in… Hold… And then release…

Remember to be in the here and now… Know that your heart is thankful and feels light when it is in the here and now…

Notice your surroundings now… Notice the passage of time… Concentrate on your breathing and the lightness of your heart… Stay with this feeling and let it fill your whole being… Continue to be in the spirit of gratitude… Continue to be thankful… And be in the here and now… Be thankful that you are in the here and now…

Now turn your attention to the day as it ends… The end of the day is drawing near… And you were able to live your life and do your work earlier… And as the day ends, it promises a tomorrow… This tomorrow is its assurance of a new beginning… And a new beginning is provided for you every single day… Be thankful for this… Feel the gratitude well up… Feel the gratitude grow on you…

You can look forward to a new day tomorrow… For tonight, it's just a matter of closing this chapter… And this exercise you are doing now—being thankful—is a wonderful nightcap for you to end another great day…

Breathe in… Hold… And then release…

Breathe in… Hold… And then release…

Breathe in… Hold… And then release…

As you exhale, say, "Thank you."

This time, make your voice louder… Make sure the world can hear you…

In a clear and audible voice, say, "Thank you."

So this ends your thankfulness meditation… Feel free to continue and you can start doing something else… Keep the spirit of gratitude burning within you… This is the spirit that makes everything light… This ends your gratitude meditation exercise…

DAY 17—DEALING WITH HEAVY EMOTIONS [20 MINUTES]

Sometimes you might feel that there are things holding you down. You might not be able to put a finger on these things—you just feel them. They're weighing heavy in your heart. Most likely, these things weighing your down are emotions. These emotions might be remnants of past or present hurts. Through meditative practice, you can enable yourself to place these emotions where they belong. Doing so might allow you the chance to move forward with your life.

Go to your comfortable spot for this exercise… You might want to lie down as things might get heavy as this exercise progresses… Wear loose and comfortable clothing… And make sure that there is nothing that can hamper your breathing…

When you're ready, you can start by closing your eyes… Try to focus on your breathing… Breathe with intentionality… Breathe with desire… Bring your whole being with you as you breathe… Focus on it and try to block out everything else, if you can… Really pour all your attention on your breathing…

Breathe in… Hold… And then release…

Breathe in… Hold… And then release…

Breathe in… Hold… And then release…

Feel your body start to relax as you put more awareness on your breathing… You can sense the rhythm of your breathing… It jives with the beating of your heart… Their motions bring another form of awareness to you… It lets you realize that you are in the here and now…

Let your body take in the relaxation… Allow this feeling to soften your stiff muscles… Allow it to unclench your fists… Allow it to unfurrow your brows… Let it ease your worries… Let it wipe away all errant thoughts…

Breathe in… Hold… And then release…

Breathe in… Hold… And then release…

Breathe in… Hold… And then release…

At this point, try to revisit the heaviness that you were feeling earlier… Is this heaviness felt in your head? Or is it prominent in your heart? Try to feel it… Try to relive the sensations… Try to bring them back… Allow it… It's the only way… As you allow them to return, you further your chances of moving on…

So let them overtake you once again… Let the heavy feelings overcome you… And feel free to let the emotions flow…

You may shed tears… cry… It's only natural…

You can shout in anger… You can bang your fist…

Go ahead and utter those curses… Feel the rage…

Or feel the frustration… Or is it guilt that you feel? Probably it's regret…

Go ahead and feel these emotions… Take your time to internalize everything… Let their weight fall on you… Let the heaviness of these emotions trample you once again…

Breathe in… Hold… And then release…

Breathe in… Hold… And then release…

Breathe in… Hold… And then release…

Bring yourself back to the here and now… Set aside those emotions for a moment… Let them stand still… Bring them to a corner and let them remain there… Know that they are not going anywhere… For this moment, this is where they will stay…

Breathe in… Hold… And then release…

Breathe in… Hold… And then release…

You are back in the here and now… In the here and now, there are no heavy feelings… In the here and now you simply exist… You are just you… to be how you should be… There are no heavy feelings in the here and now…

Get ready to go back to where you placed your heavy emotions… Prepare yourself to let go of them…

Approach the place where you left your heavy emotions… Do this slowly… Be intentional in your approach… Bring in desire with each step you take…

Breathe in… Hold… And then release…

Get ready to let go of your heavy emotions…

It's time for you to heal… It's time for you to forgive… To forgive those that hurt you… And to forgive also yourself… This is how you move on… This is how you can be rid of the weight that was pinning you down…

Imagine a body of water before you… This is the body of water where you will cast away your heavy emotions… The water will take them away… They will float away from you… Until they reach a very far place… Until they are at a safe distance… So far away that they will no longer bother you…

But first, you need to cut the cord that binds you with these emotions… Cut the string with your hand… The string is not tough to cut… Even a weak effort can cut it… So go ahead and cut… Cut away at all strings that attach you to these emotions… Break free from them…

And then cast them off to the water… One by one… Throw them to the body of water… See in your mind's eye the way you throw away these emotions… And now see the way they start to float away... They are gaining distance... And soon they are gone... Also gone are the strings that attached you to them... You can no longer feel their pull... Their weight is off your shoulders... You are free...

It's time for you to enjoy your freedom... Feel the lightness of your being now... This is how it feels when you are rid of the heavy emotions... You feel relaxed... You feel calm... You feel a certain stillness... You feel peace...

Breathe in... Hold... And then release...

Breathe in... Hold... And then release...

Breathe in... Hold... And then release...

Remain in the here and now... You have achieved your freedom... This is what the here and now gives to you... Be free in the here and now...

It's time for you to return to where you were when you started the exercise... At this point, you can start to wiggle your fingers and toes so that you can bring yourself back slowly... Enjoy the sensation of lightness that you are continuing to feel... Let your whole body delight in the pleasure... And when you're ready, open your eyes... You are now back...

DAY 18—THE DARKNESS AND INTO NOTHINGNESS [20 MINUTES]

You appreciated life and everything that comes with it in one of the earlier exercises. For this exercise, you will come to appreciate the opposite. You will come to appreciate nothingness as you focus on the darkness. For you to appreciate life's activities, you need to learn to appreciate the nothingness that comes with it. Take this journey into the darkness. You can come out with a better appreciation and understanding of life as you take the plunge into the darkness.

Find your comfortable spot once again. Settle down and try to achieve a position that is both natural and relaxing. Make sure that your position is not putting any strain on your body. Try to relax your muscles. Feel free to recline for this activity. And more importantly, make sure that all lights are off. You may want to wear a blindfold to enhance the experience.

When you are ready, you can begin your journey into darkness…

Focus on your breathing…

Breathe in… Hold… And then release…

Breathe in… Hold… And then release…

Breathe in… Hold… And then release…

Know that in the darkness, the only thing that matters is your breathing… Because it is your breathing that will bring you to the most important place and time… This place and time is where you need to be right now… You want to be in the here and now… Be in the here and now…

Breathe in… Hold… And then release…

You see nothing… Everything is dark… Let this sink in… Try to orient yourself as you take this mindfulness journey in total darkness…

In the dark, you cannot see anything… In terms of sight, there is nothing…

How does this make you feel? What sensations are brought by the darkness? Does the darkness activate your fear response just like when you were a child? Don't worry, you are in a safe place… You were always in a safe place… You're just in the here and now… And in this here and now, there's just an absence of light…

Focus on your breathing once again… Don't lose your intention and desire as you breathe…

Breathe in… Hold… And then release…

Listen to your self breathe in total darkness… Listen to the sound you make as you inhale… And as you exhale… There's a certain rhythm to it… Listen and train your ears to this rhythm… And then listen to your heart... It beats at a measured pace... Its beating coincides with your breathing... It's like they're making music... Listen to this music... Focus only on this music until you won't be able to hear anything else... Focus so that the only thing you hear is the sound coming from your breathing and your heart... Try to achieve this nothingness in total darkness...

Breathe in... Hold... And then release...

Now start to notice the sensations that are starting to present themselves in the darkness... What do you feel in the dark? Or one way to ask this is: How do you feel? Try to find the words for each sensation that you're feeling... And then just feel these sensations...

And go back to your breathing...

Breathe in... Hold... And then release...

Let each breath take away the sensations... Let each inhalation and exhalation dull your senses... It's time to let these feelings flow out of you... Allow them to leave you... Just be in the here and now...

In the here and now, you feel nothing and you see nothing... You are shrouded by darkness... This darkness also takes away the sensations... And you can hear close to nothing... The only sounds that remain are the sounds of your breathing and the sound of your heart beating...

You are experiencing nothingness... This is the experience of the nothing... Because in the here and now you are nothing...

In the here and now you exist but you are also nothing... Let your mind process the irony... This is part of the paradox of existence... in order to be, you have to be nothing first... This is where you find yourself now... This is where you start... And nothingness is where you most likely will end...

Breathe in... Hold... And then release...

Breathe in... Hold... And then release...

Breathe in... Hold... And then release...

Just continue to drift in the nothingness... Continue to be in the darkness... There is no destination... There is no sense of counting time... Do not exert any effort... Cease all deliberate acts and thoughts... There is no desire present in the state of nothingness that you find yourself in...

You float aimlessly in this nothingness... And it's perfectly alright... You don't feel any pressure... The nothingness requires nothing from you... You just need to be... You just need to exist... Exist in the nothingness—this is another paradox... You just need to be in there here and now...

Unfortunately, the nothingness that you experienced is only temporary... It is but a teaser of the ultimate nothingness that will come... Relish the thought that you were able to experience momentary nothingness... Not a lot of people can do this... And you achieved it by putting yourself in the dark...

Breathe in... Hold... And then release...

You are starting to feel something already... But your world is still dark... Allow the feelings to come back... You are already veering away from the nothingness you felt earlier... Don't worry, you will come to settle to the usual activities of life pretty soon... Soon, you will start to experience everything...

Bring awareness back to your breathing... As you hear your breath and heartbeat, try to make out the sounds that are in your periphery... As you train your ears to listen, try to also feel the sensations coming back...

Once you are ready to return you can start to open your eyes in the dark... Your eyes will start to adjust to the darkness... And pretty soon you will start to distinguish the silhouettes of the things that surround you... As you can start to see in the dark, it's time for you to get up... You may turn on the light... And you can then start to feel everything... Everything is back as it was... Everything is now ready for you to experience it once again... Try to appreciate everything a little bit more...

DAY 19—FLOATING ON WATER [20 MINUTES]

The feeling of floating on water has a restorative and relaxing effect on the body and mind. There's just something about feeling weightless that makes you feel whole again. This is the reason why several therapeutic methods are incorporating the use of water. For this exercise, you will feel the effects of how it is to be floating on water. It will be relaxing and refreshing at the same time.

For this exercise, it is best if you do this in your bathtub. You can time this exercise while you are having a dip in the tub. Or another option is to do this while swimming in a pool or at the beach. If you don't have a bathtub and if a pool or beach is out of the question, you can just imagine being immersed in water.

Get started by immersing yourself in the water. Make sure that you can lie down in the water and that you can breathe just fine. Your breathing should be unhampered when doing this exercise. Acclimatize yourself with the water. Feel your body temperature adjust itself to the temperature of the water. Start to relax your whole body. Allow your muscles to soften as they are immersed in the water. And then close your eyes…

Begin by focusing your attention on your breathing…

Breathe in… Hold… And then release…

Focus on how your body is allowing oxygen to enter it… Visualize the process in your mind… And then feel the effects as the oxygen enters your body… Feel the oxygen distributed to your bloodstream… Experience the energy it brings… Feel alive with each breath you take…

Be in the here and now… Know that you are in a safe place… The here and now is the only place and time that matters…

Try to set aside the events of the day… These events are done… They are over… They are already part of your history… Set them aside and focus on the here and now…

Do your best to ward off those errant thoughts… Those are thoughts of yesterday… Or those are thoughts of tomorrow… Maybe those are thoughts of a while ago… Or thoughts of later… These thoughts have ceased to matter or have yet to matter… They are not in the here and now…

All you need is to be in the here and now…

Breathe in… Hold… And then release…

Breathe in… Hold… And then release…

Breathe in… Hold… And then release…

Notice what is going on around you... You are surrounded by water... Imagine you are floating... Imagine that you are weightless... All your weight is being supported by the water... Its buoyancy is pushing you to the surface...

You are safe in the water... The water will not let you drown... It does its best to keep you afloat... It will simply let you be...

It even comforts you, this water... As you float, the water rocks you back and forth... It also cradles you... You are like a baby floating on this water... A baby that is rocked to sleep... The water lulls your senses... It soothes and relaxes you as it cradles you... The gentle swaying of left to right, right to left makes you feel heavenly... You start to drift into nothingness as the water rocks you to calmness and relaxation... This nothingness is the here and now...

Be in the here and now...

Breathe in... Hold... And then release...

Take all the sensations that come with the experience of floating on water... Feel the water touch you... Feel it play around you... It splashes as you make even the tiniest of movements...

You feel the water rejuvenate your tired body... It reaches all the way to your pores... It gives your skin a gentle teasing touch... And each touch brings with it a form of energy that helps you recuperate...

You now feel your energy soar... This is the effect the water has on you... It has restored you... And not only your body, but your mind as well... The coolness of the air is coupled by the warmness of the water soothes both your mind and your soul...

Now you are one with the water... You can feel your body being incorporated into the water... Your whole body is now feeling very relaxed... It just goes with the flow of things... It simply exists... It has no worries or cares... Because water knows not these things... Water is simply water... It flows and takes the shape of its container... That is the nature of water... And that is how you feel now... Let this feeling take over you... Let the feeling of being one with the water overcome you... You are one with it and you are in the here and now...

Breathe in... Hold... And then release...

Feel the gentleness of water as you imagine yourself transformed into a liquid state... It is cool... It refreshes... It is soothing... But also know of water's potential for great power... This is the magnificence of water... It brings life... It refreshes... It soothes and cools... And yet it can be a source of power... It can be a source of greatness... And think of its abundance... Water is everywhere... The world is full of it... Even parts of your body are made up of water...

Continue to float... Continue to feel the calmness as you drift along... Know that you do not need any direction... You have no aim, no purpose... You simply need to be... To be in the here and now... You achieve this as you float... Continue to float... Be one with the water...

Breathe in... Hold... And then release...

Breathe in... Hold... And then release...

Breathe in... Hold... And then release...

And now it's time to come back... Time to end your floating in water... Bring yourself back gently... Start to let your senses come back... Re-acclimatize yourself to your surroundings... Continue to feel the water surrounding your body... Move your body just a little bit... You should be making small splashes as you do this... Feel and hear these splashes that you are making... And when you're ready, open your eyes...

DAY 20—THE CANDLE MEDITATION EXERCISE [25 MINUTES]

A candle meditation exercise is one of the most calming exercises in this book. What sets this exercise apart is that your focus and attention is diverted to something in front of you—the candle. It is easier to let go of your thoughts as you pour your focus and attention towards the candle. With the physical presence of the candle and the light of the fire, this exercise will let you reach a deeper level of mindfulness. Practicing the candle meditation exercise is one sure-fire way to improve your concentration.

There's a bit of preparation needed as you start this exercise. Prepare the room you will be in. And then also prepare a candle and something to light the candle with. Take a few minutes to prepare the whole space before you light the candle. Distribute your good energy all over the space. Shower it with your presence. Turn off the lights (or you can just turn them down). This exercise is much easier to do in the dark. Too much light in the room will dampen the mood.

Light the candle and settle down. Feel comfortable as you settle in your position. The best position for this exercise is sitting down and having the light of the candle at eye level. You may position your head a little lower if you wish. Just make sure that your head is not settled at a weird angle. Also make sure that your back is not slumping.

Feel the relaxation overtake all the other sensations… Settle in and get even more comfortable… Look at the light of the candle… Let the light contrast with the darkness of the room… Try to also be aware of your periphery… This is the darkness that surrounds you… And in front of you is a light source… The candle…

Continue by bringing your attention to your breathing… Put in your whole self as you breathe… Inhale and exhale with desire and intentness…

Breathe in… Hold… And then release…

Maintain your contact with the candle as you breathe… Connect with the light… See the light of the candle with intentness and desire… Continue to breathe naturally as you do this… Focus on the light… while you maintain the rhythm of your breathing…

Breathe in… Hold… And then release…

Breathe in… Hold… And then release…

Breathe in… Hold… And then release…

You are in the here and now… In the here and now it is dark… Darkness covers the room you are in… But in the here and now there is light in front of you… The light is small but it illuminates the room… It fills the room with its presence…

As such, this light also fills you with its presence… It is small… It's just a flicker in the vastness of the place you are in… But it is enough to bring you some awareness of the room you are in… It is enough to bring your awareness to the here and now…

Breathe in… Hold… And then release…

Breathe in… Hold… And then release…

Breathe in… Hold… And then release…

See the fire on the wick of the candle… See the motion it does… You can see it dancing… As if it has a life of its own… As if it has motivation from within… Wanting you to watch it… So it dances… It flickers… It sways back and forth… But it never leaves the wick of the candle…

You can start to feel a little bit of heat… This is the heat coming from the fire of the candle… This heat is just enough for you to distinguish it in the coldness of the room… You feel its warmth… It is a welcome feeling… You let this warmth enrich you… You let the sensations flow to your body… You relish it… It's a wonderful feeling to feel the warmth of the candle…

Breathe in… Hold… And then release…

Breathe in… Hold… And then release…

Imagine that each breath brings life to the fire… Imagine it is your breathing that is powering the fire of the candle… You can actually see the fire dance more furtively as you inhale and exhale… This is your capacity to give life to others… Like your breath on the candle, your spirit is capable of touching others in ways that will motivate and inspire them… Continue to give life to the candle… Breathe with intent and desire… And then absorb the energies of the candle as you breathe… It also gives you spirit… It makes you feel alive… Let the candle help you experience the here and now…

Be in the here and now… Focus on the candle… In the here and now, all you have is the darkness around you and the light of the candle in front of you…

Breathe in… Hold… And then release…

Breathe in… Hold… And then release…

Now start to notice the rest of the things that the light and fire touches… Notice your periphery start to become just a little bit visible… It is the light of the candle that is making this happen… Notice also the melted wax of the candle… See it melt… See it drip on the sides of the candle… And notice how the wick holds the fire… The wick is steady… It does not disintegrate even with the great heat of the fire… Notice these things… These are the effects of the candle…

And now it's time to dig deeper and start to feel the sensations and emotions that the candle brings… What can you feel in the darkness? And what can you feel with the light of the candle? Feel the sensations that the candle brings in consonance with the darkness… Feel also the emotions… Let them swirl and capture you… Let these emotions become one with you…

Focus on the light of the candle… Focus on the heat that the fire gives… Feel it and feel yourself live… This is your life… The light and the fire represent your life… This is the message of the candle… Let it remind you of how it is to live… Let it remind you to be in the here and now…

Be in the here and now… In the here and now you burn bright… In the here and now you give off warmth… In the here and now you give off energy… The energy you give off is your spirit… Let your spirit burn bright… So that others can see it more clearly… Let your spirit radiate warmth… So that others can feel and appreciate your presence more… Live life like a candle… Live life like a candle that burns in the here and now…

Breathe in… Hold… And then release…

Breathe in… Hold… And then release…

Breathe in… Hold… And then release…

You are now feeling calm… The stillness and warmth is making you feel very relaxed… Stay with this feeling and maintain your gaze on the candle… See the candle for what it is… Appreciate it… Take in its beauty, its form, its function… And let the message of the candle echo in your mind…

As you are ready to return, close your eyes… Appreciate the darkness as you keep your eyes closed… You are about to end your candle meditation… When you're ready to end the exercise, blow out your candle… Continue to feel the sensations… Continue to feel relaxed and calm… You may take a few moments to lie down and let your mind and body re-acclimatize to your environment…

DAY 21—GUIDED MEDITATION FOR DEEP SLEEP [30 MINUTES]

Sleep has become such a luxury these days because that even the rich and famous are getting so few of it. And a lot of people are foregoing sleep in favor of work or play. It seems sleep now is getting to be the new hot commodity. But you can actually get a good night's sleep if you wish to. It shouldn't be that hard. You can achieve the required number of hours of slumber per day. All you need to do is to put your mind to it. Your mind is very powerful, and it also needs to rest. This is what sleep gives to your mind. And know that your mind is powerful enough to will itself to sleep. Take the time to practice this deep sleep meditation exercise. You will be doing the body scanning technique to bring you to la-la land in no time.

Start by readying your bedroom for sleep. Make sure your bed is ready. Also make sure that the room is conducive for sleeping. Try to achieve peace and quiet for the night. Turn off or turn down the lights. Change to your pajamas or your sleepwear. Get into a very comfortable position. Get under the covers and get ready to start your meditation.

As you got your surroundings ready, now it's time to get yourself prepared… You have to get ready for sleep. Lie down and achieve a very comfortable position… Adjust your position if you need to… Toss and turn until you achieve the perfect position for sleep… Close your eyes… Start to relax… Let your body slump to the mattress… Start feeling the gentle caress of your sheets… Feel your body adjust to the temperature of the room…

As you achieve this, it's time to take control of your breathing… Bring your awareness to your breathing…

Breathe in… Hold… And then release…

Breathe in… Hold… And then release…

Breathe in… Hold… And then release…

Be methodical in your breathing… Bring in your intentionality with each breath… Take it slow… Let the calmness of your slow breaths reach you… Bring in relaxation and calm with each breath… Start to feel the warm fuzzy sensations… Relax and be calm…

Breathe in… Hold… And then release…

Bring yourself to the most important place and time… This place and time is where you need to be as you get yourself ready for sleep… Be in the here and now… Know deep down inside of you that there is nothing you need to do right now… You just need to breathe calmly. Drift and go with the flow… Let the feeling of sleepiness start to take control… every breath brings sleep closer and closer…

Breathe in… Hold… And then release…

Be in the here and now... Welcome the sleepiness... Allow sleep to touch you... Let it do its magic on your mind and body...

At this point, try to deliberately release your breaths ever more slowly... Take a long and deep breath...

Breathe in... Slowly...

Hold...

And then release... very slowly... Punctuate the release with intent and desire...

Try to prolong the release... Feel even more relaxed as you do so...

And then continue with the pattern... Maintain the rhythm of your breathing... Still breathe with the desire and intentness... Continue to be in the here and now...

Breathe in... Hold... And then release...

You are calm... You are relaxed... Everything around you is quiet... You are shrouded by the darkness that is safe and comforting... You can start to feel the warm touch of sleep...

Continue to feel the relaxation and slowly scan your body... Start from your head and slowly move downward... See your body with your mind's eye... Visualize your forehead, your eyes, your nose, your mouth, your chin... See these parts of your face and head in your mind... Until you reach your neck and shoulders... Observe each part... And then feel the sensations... Take your sweet time... You are in no hurry...

Move your scanning downward... And continue to feel the sensations... Take note of the sensations that you are experiencing while you scan your body...

Arrive at the center of your body... Settle your scan at the level of your stomach and chest, your solar plexus... This is your core... Scan its entirety... Notice your chest and diaphragm's movement... See how they gently rise and fall with your breathing... And continue to feel the sensations.... Remember to not be in a hurry... Take your time as you observe your body...

Breathe in... Hold... And then release...

Now reach the level of your hips... You are now scanning your lower torso... Notice your hips and groin area... See your upper legs... See if you can make out the tiny imperceptible movements that they make... Or just observe their stillness... What sensations do you feel?

Move lower and start to scan your legs... Scan the upper part of it... And then move to your knees... Slowly go down and observe your shin... And then your calf... Go further and you can now scan your feet... Scan even the soles of your feet... These are the legs and feet that held you up the entire day... What sensations do you feel? Be deliberate in your scanning... You want to observe every aspect of your legs... And you want to feel all the sensations... Do this slowly... You can take your time scanning...

Breathe in... Hold... And then release...

And then you can move to your arms... Scan your upper arm... See the muscles of your arm and notice how they are working as you are in the clutches of sleep... Move your way to your hands... Marvel at their beauty... These are the hands that enabled you to do wonderful and meaningful work... What sensations do you feel? Scan your arms and hands slowly... Be deliberate in your scanning... Go ahead, you can take your time...

Go back to the sensations that you felt as you scanned your body... Which parts did you feel tension and tightness? And which parts were most relaxed? Go back to the areas where you felt relaxed... Imagine the feeling of relaxation moving to the other parts... Imagine this relaxation start to invade the tight and tense areas... Let this wonderful feeling pervade... Let relaxation permeate... Let it cover your entire body... Start on the areas with the sensations of calmness and relaxation and let them work their way to the rest of the parts...

Breathe in... Hold... And then release...

Be in the here and now... In the here and now you are calm and relaxed... In the here and now you are very close to sleep... Edging closer by the second... So near you can already feel it....

Breathe in... Hold... And then release...

Now your body is in its most relaxed state... This is what it means to get yourself ready for sleep... Your body is allowing itself to welcome sleep... It is making your body hospitable for sleep... So that sleep can stay longer... So that sleep can work its magic on you... So that you can achieve the deepest and most relaxing sleep...

Your head is feeling ever so light... You can start to feel a delightful sensation on your head... This is sleep making your feel very comfortable... It is starting to work its magic on you... Your whole body is feeling very relaxed... There's no tightness... There's no tension... Your body scan released all the tightness and tension... You just feel light right now... You feel like you are floating on air... You are drifting off to slumber... You are gently being carried by sleep to the land of dreams...

Breathe in... Hold... And then release...

Be in the here and now... The here and now you are in looks very much like a restful state of slumber... The here and now is also a very comforting and relaxing place... It is moving you ever so close to true tranquility... You are very close to achieving the sleep that you desire... You are on your way there... Just a little more and you can have a firm grasp of it...

Breathe in... Hold... And then release...

You are safe and sound where you are... As you drift off to sleep you are filled with such a sense of delight and security... Nothing matters anymore... Everything turns to blank...

Now you can sense the nothingness... Your sense of hearing is slowly drifting away as well... Everything is dark... You feel nothing but warmth, calmness, and relaxation... The world you know is starting to melt away... Welcome to nothingness... Welcome to sleep... Sleep well... Reach into the farthest depths of sleep... Goodnight... Sleep tight...

DAY 22—SELF-HEALING MEDITATION [30 MINUTES]

You will once again tap the power of your mind to allow your body to heal. This is one of the mind's superpowers. And you can use this time and time again to bring you to the brink of health. This self-healing meditation is especially useful if ailments and disease are troubling you. It may not totally take away the pain or heal your right away, but the act of meditating will prime both your mind and body for healing. One benefit of this exercise is that you will instantly feel a little bit better. And sometimes it's just a matter of setting the mood so that you can start to activate your body's self-healing process.

As always, start by settling into your sweet spot. This is the third week of your meditation practice. You should have established your sweet spot by now. Go to this place and start getting comfortable. Place your body in a relaxed position… Let it achieve stillness and calm… You will need this in order for your body to heal…

Once you achieve the relaxed pose, start by bringing your awareness to your breathing… Let all your energy flow through your breathing… Concentrate on it and execute each breath like you mean it… Let air flow in and out of you with great desire… Focus your mind on your body's process of respiration…

Breathe in… Hold… And then release…

Breathe in… Hold… And then release…

Breathe in… Hold… And then release…

Imagine that each breath you take is a cleansing breath… It brings in positive energy… And this positive energy enlivens every cell in your body… It makes your muscles feel more relaxed… And the air you breathed in actually sweeps away the tension and tightness… And as you exhale, it takes with it all the impurities of your body… Your body is cleansed and purified with each breath you take…

Breathe in… Hold… And then release…

Be in the here and now… Let your breathing be the only thing that matters… Let your breathing bring you to the here and now… Allow it to block off all the distractions… Allow it to be the only focus you have… Because breathing is bringing you the good energy… Breathing is what allows your body to be cleansed and purified… This is the reality of the here and now…

Now begin to observe your body… Try to feel the sensations… What is your body trying to tell you? Are there specific parts that call out to you? Where are these parts? Can you try to identify them?

Breathe in… Hold… And then release…

What are they trying to tell you? Are you sensing some discomfort in these parts? Or worse, are you feeling pain? Is there something wrong with that body part? Is it not functioning well enough? What is stopping these parts from being at their best? Try to feel these sensations… Feel what these body parts are feeling… Don't be afraid of them… They are part of you anyway…

Feel the discomfort… Feel the pain… Know that they are part of you… There's a reason why they're there… There's a reason why you're feeling them right now… This is part of the here and now… Go ahead and feel them… Experience every sensation….

Now go back to your breathing…

Breathe in… Hold… And then release…

Breathe in… Hold… And then release…

Breathe in… Hold… And then release…

Bring your awareness back to the air that surrounds you… This is the cleansing and purifying air… This is the air that is needed for your body to start its healing process… Appreciate the fact that this cleansing and purifying air is all around you… It is yours for the taking… All you have to do is to want it… So be deliberate in your breathing… Desire every breath… Make sure you get all the air you need… So that your body can start healing… So that your mind can also start healing…

Breathe in… Hold… And then release…

Breathe in… Slowly…

Hold… Make sure to let the air circulate inside you…

And then release… Very slowly once again… Let your exhalation bring out the discomfort and pain that you are feeling…

Now feel the cleansing and purifying air start to work their way on your feet… They start at your soles and you can feel them on your toes… There's a warm feeling to them… It tingles… And it tickles a bit… You enjoy the feeling… It is in stark contrast to the pain and discomfort you felt in the other areas…

This warm, wonderful feeling starts to spread… It starts to move its way up… You can now feel it on your legs… And it somehow starts to take away some of the discomfort and pain… This energy is slowly substituting all the bad sensations… It is replacing it with a certain kind of warmth…

The pain and discomfort are still there… It did not go away entirely… But the energy is trying to make it more tolerable… You can stand the pain and discomfort now… Its intensity has greatly diminished… It makes you feel all the more relaxed… You appreciate being momentarily released from the clutches of pain and discomfort…

It feels liberating… And you want it to continue… And this energy, the air that you breathe is moving once again… It reaches your lower torso and it does its magic there also… The pain and discomfort are waning… You start to feel whole again… You are now reminiscing the time when you were at your peak health-wise….

Breathe in… Hold… And then release…

Breathe in… Hold… And then release…

Breathe in… Hold… And then release…

Start to feel this energy rising above your ankles, flowing up your lower legs… And then it reaches your knees…. Until it makes its way up to your upper legs… Allow the relaxation that the energy brings to continue to spread throughout your body… It is now trying to reach your hips… Soon you can feel it reach your pelvis… And then it settles on your stomach…

You continue to take in all the positivity from this… You are enjoying the feeling of having the discomfort and pain subside… You look forward to having more of it… You know that the air you take in is promising you more relief… You know you can look forward to more healing and recovery… Your body is actually starting to heal…

From your stomach, it is now making its way to your chest… And then you can start to feel it on your back… It is hitting your core… It is bringing you back the balance you once lost… You can feel whole again… All these feelings of healing and recovery are being brought about by the air you breathe… Continue to bring in desire with every breath…

Breathe in… Hold… And then release…

It flows now to your arms… It has made its way up to your elbows… You can start to feel the energy bring its vibe to your wrist… Soon your hands and filled with this energy… It spreads even to your fingers… It is starting to cover your entire body… And the delightful sensations just put you in a more relaxed state… Let the calmness take over…

Now this healing energy that comes from the air you breathe is making its way to its final destination… It slowly climbs up to your head… You can now feel the muscles of your face start to soften… You are now smiling… This is the effect of healing on you… Your neck and shoulders are also very relaxed now…

You can feel it in your eyes now… Even if your eyes are closed, you can feel it… It touches your eyelids as it makes its way ever upward… And now it settles on your forehead… You can feel the energy hover above your head now… You can sense its warmth as it tries to decompress all the unnecessary thoughts… It is also healing your mind now… You can feel a certain lightness overtake you… This is the lightness that is borne out of healing… And you heal yourself as you breathe… You are bringing the healing energy inside your body with each breath you take…

Breathe in… Hold… And then release…

Breathe in… Hold… And then release…

Breathe in… Hold… And then release…

Be in the here and now… The here and now is the time and place where healing can take place… Stay in this moment… And know that you can go to this place and time anytime you wish… Know that your body is capable of healing itself… All you need is the time and place… All you need to do is to be in the here and now…

Maintain the relaxing feeling you have established as your body is trying to heal itself... Feel jubilant at your body's great ability to heal, recharge, and recuperate... Continue to feel the calm... Continue to feel at ease... Maintain that confidence you feel right now as you are allowing your body to heal...

You are now ready to return... Feel free to shake off the relaxation a bit by doing some slight movements... This will bring life back to your relaxed muscles... You can even do some stretching poses... And if you are ready, you can open your eyes...

Or feel free to maximize your current blissful feeling... You can continue to feel relaxed and calm... You can also continue to let your body heal a little bit more... Know that this process takes time... It is best to let your healing continue... It should not be rushed... This process should be unhurried...

DAY 23—STRESS RELIEF MEDITATION: LOOKING AT THE STARS [30 MINUTES]

Another wonder that's always available to us is the stars. They should be visible and bright on a clear night. The stars give you a sense of awe. There is a mystery to them that awakens the curious mind. This mystery and wonder have transfixed a lot of people to the night sky, hoping to catch a glimpse of the constellation of stars. By looking up in the night sky, you can attain a form of peace. You can gaze to the stars and appreciate them in their majestic beauty and splendor. Try this meditation exercise tonight.

You need to be outdoors for this exercise. It is with great hope that the weather will cooperate. Go out under the night sky and find for yourself a place where you can be seated comfortably. Or, if you prefer, you can lie down for this exercise. Find a place that is dark so that you can get a better view of the stars. Settle down and get yourself in your most comfortable position.

Let your eyes adjust to the darkness as you become more comfortable in your position. Feel the night breeze try to cool you down… And try to distance yourself from the noise that you may hear on your periphery… Detach yourself from the world… Now it's just you and the night sky… And the sky is offering you thousands, if not millions, of stars… They are all right there above you… Behold the stars of the night sky…

As you take in the view of the stars, try to gain awareness of your breathing… Be aware of how the air flows in and out of your body… Try to visualize their path as they enter and leave your body… Be deliberate in your breathing… Try to put your whole self into your breathing…

Breathe in… Hold… And then release…

Breathe in… Hold… And then release…

Breathe in… Hold… And then release…

Maintain your focus on the sky and the stars as you breathe… Let the air around you energize you… Visualize its flow… See with your mind's eye how the air is entering your body… See how it circulates inside of you… And then see it leave you… Watch the air as it returns to its starting point…

Breathe in… Take a look at the sky… Appreciate its vastness… Try to fathom what you can see before you… Try to fathom how vast it is… Try and see if you can comprehend its limitlessness…

Hold your breath for a few moments… See the stars… There are a myriad stars out before you…

And then release… A million tiny specs of light out there in the vastness of space… See them twinkle, see them shine, see them sparkle… The night sky comes alive with the stars out and about… They are like a hundred thousand diamonds on the night sky… Their tiny but powerful light punctuates the darkness of space…

Be deliberate in the way you breathe... Bring in all of your energy into your breathing... Let your whole being breathe with you... And as you do, appreciate the beauty of the darkened sky that is above you... Desire every breath you take... And use this same desire in your observation and appreciation of the stars...

Breathe in... Hold... And then release...

See the stars up above... Watch how they brighten the sky up above you... It's not totally black... You can see the light of the moon... And you can see the light of the stars...

These stars are twinkling... All stars flicker... Their interplay of light and dark makes it seem like they are blinking... And you can faintly see different colors as the stars sparkle... Try to make out the yellows and the oranges... And the reds and the purples... And even the blues... Try to spot a star giving out a blue twinkle...

See the majesty of the constellation... This is the same constellation your forefathers viewed... This is the same night sky your ancestors saw when they looked up... Appreciate this fact... Appreciate the fact that you have something you can share with your forefathers and ancestors... The night sky has always been there... It's been there through time... And will always be there in the days to come...

Let the night sky remind you of the here and now... Let the darkness of night bring you to the only place and time that matters... Let the light of the stars that dance on the dark canvass of the sky remind you that the only place and time you need to at is the here and now...

Be in the here and now... This is what the night sky is telling you... This is the message the stars are trying to impress on you... Remember that they have been there since the dawn of time... And as always, the night sky and the stars remain there... To your eyes, they will always be in the here and now... Even though they are quite far... so far away... and they are from another time... a distance so far...

But be in the here and now... And look at the stars as they twinkle... Relive the time when you were a child... Remember the old nursery rhyme...

Look up the night sky and start to wonder... Wonder what they are... Think about the stars and what they mean to you... Think about them because they are trying to tell a story... They are sending a message to you...

Be in the here and now as you gaze at the stars... And let the stars do their nightly light performance...

Breathe in... Hold... And then release...

Breathe in... Hold... And then release...

Breathe in... Hold... And then release...

Now feel the sensation that is entering your body... What feelings are starting to feel? Can you feel the calm and stillness that the night sky and stars are giving? Try to let the view relax you... It is a view of peace... It should make you feel at ease... You are watching a spectacle of light... Appreciate the interplay of light and dark as you gaze at the night sky...

Experience wave after wave of rejuvenating energy flow through you... This is the effect of the calm and stillness that you are feeling... This is what the stars of the night offer you... Let it whisper in your ear that nothing matters... Nothing matters in the here and now... All you have to do is to look up... All you have to do is to keep your eyes open... And see the stars... See them shine brightly... Like a thousand tiny diamonds in the sky...

Breathe in... Hold... And then release...

Breathe in... Hold... And then release...

Breathe in... Hold... And then release...

Continue to be amazed at what you are seeing... Feel the joy that this spectacle brings... Count yourself lucky that you can open your eyes and see the stars... Feel blessed at being able to go out at night and be right under the stars...

Bask in the light of the night sky... Let the light that illuminates the darkness of night bathe you... Feel its presence... Feel its power... Let it transport you to the here and now... This is the power of the light of the night sky... Let the sparkling dazzling light bring you to the only place and time that matters...

Be in the here and now...

Revel in the stillness and the calm...

Appreciate the light show in front of you...

The stars are out tonight... And they dance... They burn brightly... They do this for you... So that you are reminded of your existence... So that you can once again bring yourself to the here and now...

Try to look at the stars more intently this time... Etch them to memory... Try to see their image even as you close your eyes... Let their light continue to shine even with your eyes closed...

And then just take a moment... Pause... Take a moment to be with the night sky... Take a moment to be with the stars... Take a moment to be in the here and now... Pause... And take your time... You are in no hurry... The stars are in no hurry as well... They have existed for eons... And they will continue to exist for eons more... They are not going anywhere... So just take it in... Take all of it in...

Breathe in... Hold... And then release...

Breathe in... Hold... And then release...

Breathe in... Hold... And then release...

Once you are ready to return, open your eyes... Move your arms and legs... You can even do some light stretches... Bring your senses back by putting some form of motion to your body...

You can once again see the beauty of the night sky and the stars... Feel free to stay where you are... You can continue to gaze at the stars... Again, there is no need to hurry... You can take your time... Tonight, it's just you and the stars...

DAY 24—BEFORE SLEEP DEEP RELAXATION MEDITATION: REFLECTING ON YOUR JOURNEY [30 MINUTES]

It's always advisable to take the time to reflect on your life. You can gain a lot of insight as you continue your journey. And it is also refreshing and relaxing to do as well. This exercise can be done just as you are about to sleep. The lightness of the mood you will be experiencing while doing this exercise will help bring you pleasant sleep. Prepare yourself for a night of relaxing and restful slumber.

First, prepare your bedroom. It's always best to make sure that your rest area is conducive to sleep. Set the temperature of the room just right—not too cold, not to warm. Turn off the lights or you can just dim them if you are uncomfortable with total darkness. Wear your sleep clothes—clothing that is loose and that will allow your body to be comfortable.

Settle into your bed and try to attain a very comfortable position… Go ahead and toss and turn a little bit… Try to find that sweet spot… Try to achieve the perfect position… Once you feel relaxed and calm, you may begin with the exercise… Close your eyes…

Feel the stillness of the bedroom… Realize that it is late at night… The world is also calling it a day… It's time for rest… It's time for you to go to sleep…

You find yourself in a very comfortable space… You are in your bedroom… You are lying down in your bed… You know these spaces very well… These are safe spaces… These spaces allow you to rest… So go ahead and let your weary mind and body rest…

Try to focus on your breathing… Let your breathing bring you relaxation… Let it bring you calmness… Let your breathing create stillness in your mind and body…

Breathe in… Hold… And then release…

Each breath is a breath of relaxation… You are taking in relaxation… Take more of it…

Breathe in… Hold… And then release…

You feel more and more relaxed… You can sense a certain warmth that tries to envelop your whole body… The air you breathe is letting this warm feeling spread all throughout your body… Your muscles now feel loose… There is nary a sign of tension in them… The tightness you earlier felt is all but gone… Your whole body now feels light… It feels like you are floating on air… And that your body is perched on a soft fluffy cloud which is your bed…

Let these feelings run through you… Enjoy the sensations… These are the sensations of relaxation… These feelings are brought about as you take in more of the relaxing air you breathe…

Breathe in… Hold… And then release…

Breathe in... Hold... And then release...

Breathe in... Hold... And then release...

As you continue to enjoy the wonderful sensations, try to bring yourself to the here and now... Let your breathing help you with this... The here and now is where you want to be... It is the only place and time that matters...

Realize that you are calm and still in the here and now... Realize that you have decided to set aside all cares and worries... You do not need those in the here and now... You can set them aside for now because they have no place as you sleep... As you try to attain peaceful slumber, you only need to be present... Just be in the here and now...

Breathe in... Hold... And then release...

Breathe in... Hold... And then release...

Breathe in... Hold... And then release...

Nothing else matters in the here and now... It is just you and your breathing... It is just you feeling very relaxed... very still... very calm...

And now it's time to think about your life... Reflect on your journey... Try to bring back all of your achievements as you traversed through the road of life ... Take the time to relive and remember these memories...

Know that you have accomplished a lot... And know that you have a lot more to accomplish... Think about these accomplishments for a moment... Try to bring yourself back when these happened... Relish at the joy you felt when you experienced these accomplishments... See in your mind's eye how happy you were then...

And then think of the people that helped you get to where you are right now... These are the people that are important to you... These are the people that matter... Fill your heart with gratitude as you try to conjure their images in your mind... Be thankful that you crossed paths with these individuals... As they made an impact on you, you also made an impact on them....

Get a good sense of how wonderful your life has been, even with all the ups and downs... The fact that you are breathing is already a testament to life's greatness... The fact that you can be in the here and now means that your existence matters... Try to capture the entirety of the greatness of your existence in your thoughts...

Dwell on the positives... And know that you will have more opportunities in store for you tomorrow... For tomorrow is another day...

Realize that your struggles and challenges have a purpose... This is part of your journey... They give more meaning to your life... Take these in as well... Let these struggles and challenges enrich you... Take them wholeheartedly and also appreciate them...

Breathe in... Hold... And then release...

Fill your heart with gladness and content as you reflect on your journey… Your journey thus far has put you in the most important spot—the here and now… The here and now offers boundless opportunities… There are countless more chapters to write in the book of life…

But those are for another day… Right now, what is important is that you are filled with a spirit of gratitude… You took the time to reflect and it has brought you to a place and time that is filled with longing and love… Enjoy this moment… Put these thoughts in the backseat… You can always look at the rear-view mirror to see these thoughts… This is how you reflect on your life…

Return to the here and now… But know that you can always glance at the rear-view mirror… Do this if you want to reflect on the life you lived thus far… But right now, be in the here and now… Achieve this with your breathing…

Breathe in… Hold… And then release…

Breathe in… Hold… And then release…

Breathe in… Hold… And then release…

In the here and now everything is still… The night is still… The world is still… Your body is still… and so is your mind… Your heart is filled with joy and gratitude… In the here and now, you are ready for sleep…

So welcome sleep… You can let go of wakefulness now… It's time for you to rest… Welcome sleep and let it be part of your here and now…

Breathe in… Hold… And then release…

Breathe in… Hold… And then release…

Each breath is making you feel more relaxed… Each breath brings you closer to sleep…

Breathe in… Hold… And then release…

Breathe in… Hold… And then release…

Allow yourself to drift to sleep… Loosen your grip with the conscious waking world… You can let go of it now… You were awake for much of the day… You devoted the majority of your time to achieve your goals… It's time to rest… It's time to let your body recuperate… It's time to let your mind decompress…

But maintain the feeling of calmness and joy… Let the positivity continue to surround you… These feelings will bring you a kind of sleep that is more restful… It will allow you to go deeper and deeper into your sleep… This is the sleep that you want… This is the sleep that you deserve… So claim it… Prime yourself for deep sleep… Prepare yourself for a night of truly restful slumber…

Breathe in… Hold… And then release…

Breathe in… Hold… And then release…

Breathe in… Hold… And then release…

What matters now is just you drifting off to unconsciousness with a thankful heart… This is the here and now that you find yourself in…

Release your grip of consciousness… Give in to sleep…

This meditation exercise is about to end… It will end at the count of 3…

3…

2…

1…

Good night…

DAY 25—RELAXED MINDFUL EATING: GUIDED MINDFULNESS TO APPRECIATE YOUR MEAL BETTER [30 MINUTES]

This is a special exercise that will break your usual dining routine. Mindful eating is getting to be more popular nowadays. This experience will bring you closer to the food that you are eating. You can prepare a special meal or just a simple one. Know that the type of food or dish does not matter much in this exercise. This is all about the journey. Getting to your desired destination will just be the icing on the cake—a cherry to top this proverbial sundae. This is all about learning to appreciate the food you are eating—the meal you are partaking in—through mindfulness. You can experience a higher level of delight and satisfaction with your food if you are more mindful of it.

To start with, make sure that you have everything prepared. The easiest would be to order food from a restaurant. But you can also cook and prepare your own food for this exercise. Cooking your own food will bring a deeper mindfulness dimension into this whole experience. Settle down on the table and get yourself in a comfortable position. Get ready to start your mindful eating journey.

You can start by connecting your breath and body…

Breathe in… Hold… And then release…

Get a full sense of how your body is feeling right at this very moment… Become aware of the sensations that are coursing through you… Become aware as well of the many behaviors your body is doing at this point… Notice the tiny gestures, the twitches, or even the grumbling of your stomach… These are the usual reactions to hunger… You must surely be manifesting these reactions by now…

Next, try to dig deep and notice the emotions that you are feeling at this very moment… How do you feel inside? Do you feel the anticipation? Do feel the excitement? What thoughts and feelings do you have right now knowing that you are about to partake in a meal? Take the time to feel and to let these emotions emerge…

Breathe in… Hold… And then release…

Keep your body and breath connected… Stay conscious of this… This will allow you to stay in the here and now… You need to be in the here and now to be mindful of your meal… This will let you appreciate your meal more…

Be in the here and now…

You must be feeling very hungry now… The anticipation is building… Tune in to this awareness of hunger… Can you feel the pangs? How about thirst? Do you feel the need to drink? What thoughts dominate your mind right now? Try to understand the act of eating and drinking… And further this understanding by asking yourself why you are eating what you eat… And why you are drinking what you drink… Take time to ask these things…. And take time to answer…

Know the purpose of your meal... Is it merely sustenance? Or is there something more to this meal than just for food and drink to fill you? Is this meal a journey into pleasure? Is this meal about making you feel good inside and out? Or is there a social aspect to the meal? Are you enjoying the meal with people? Who are these people? And why do they matter?

Go ahead and think of these things... Let these thoughts marinate... Let them enhance your experience as you partake in your meal...

Breathe in... Hold... And then release...

It's time to eat... But before doing so, try to handle the food that's in front of you... Go ahead and touch it... Take it... Put it on your palm... Hold the food... Try to let your curiosity run wild as you hold this piece of gastronomical delight... Observe with all your senses everything about it... From its shape, size, color, texture... Observe it...

And then become aware of the sensations and feelings that come about from your observation... How does this make you feel? How does it feel to put the food you eat on your hands? Take some time to think about this...

Breathe in... Hold... And then release...

It's time to taste the food... Go ahead and put it in your mouth... Be very deliberate when you do this... As you put it in your mouth, let its aroma tickle your nose... Let its fine odor enhance your experience... Its aroma is supposed to heighten your other senses...

Breathe in... Hold... And then release...

Try to let the food touch your lips first... Let its warm temperature kiss your lips as you start to put it inside your mouth... And once it is inside your mouth, take the time to really taste it... Taste it for all its worth... Let the flavors burst in your mouth... Let your tongue marvel at the wonderful sensations it is feeling...

What flavors can you sense? What different textures are present in your mouth right now? Go ahead and name them all... Feel a certain form of satisfaction emerge as you experience all the different flavors and textures in your mouth...

Start chewing the food... Feel more bursts of flavor as your teeth and mouth do their work of breaking the food down... Chew slowly... Make sure that you can really experience all the wonderful flavors of the food... Appreciate as well the changes in texture as you chew...

And then when the food has been broken down to a much smaller piece, swallow it... Let it dance around your throat as you swallow... And when it finally settles down in your stomach, feel the delight... You have just eaten mindfully... You took the time and effort to really appreciate the food that you are eating...

Breathe in... Hold... And then release... Remember to be in the here and now... In the here and now you are being nourished by nutritious and delicious food... And you appreciate every morsel... You took the time to bring out all the goodness in it... Each bite, each chew, each swallow has become such a delightful experience...

Breathe in... Hold... And then release...

And as the food settles in your stomach, take time to appreciate its journey... Realize that the food you see in front of you now underwent several transformations... It went through a process of preparation... And now it has been transformed into a delightful dish that you can enjoy to your heart's content... Appreciate your food's journey from farm to table...

Also appreciate the hands that shaped and formed the food you have before you... These hands belong to hardworking people... These are the farmers, delivery persons, cooks... These people were instrumental in bringing that delicious dish that is in front of you right now... Appreciate these loving hands...

Breathe in... Hold... And then release...

Take another bite... Go ahead and eat once again... What memories were conjured as you ate the food? Did it bring you back to your childhood? Were memories of the past brought back as you bit into your food? Or did it bring other more recent memories? Know that food has this power... Food can connect the past to the present... Take the time to relive these memories through the food you eat... Let past happiness re-emerge each time you partake of the food...

Breathe in... Hold... And then release...

Go ahead and build a steady rhythm of eating... Eat slow... Take the time to really appreciate each morsel of food you put in your mouth... This is how to eat mindfully... And it is a wonderful way to eat... Does your food taste much better if you are more mindful of it? Enjoy the sensations... Reminisce about the happy memories it brought... And let it nourish you... Let it remind you that life is great... Let it remind you that you are here to live... You are here to live in the here and now...

And in the here and now you are being nourished by wonderful and delicious food... Food that was methodically and meticulously prepared by hardworking and loving hands... Food that brings back memories—happy memories... This is the here and now...

Breathe in... Hold... And then release...

Breathe in... Hold... And then release...

Breathe in... Hold... And then release...

Remain in the here and now for the course of your meal...

You are now at the conclusion of your mindfulness eating exercise... But go ahead and continue with your meal... Eat heartily... Eat with joy... And eat slowly... Maintain mindfulness with each bite... Food tastes so much better this way... Bon appetit!

DAY 26—MORNING ANXIETY-REDUCING MEDITATION TO KICK-START YOUR DAY [30 MINUTES]

Mornings are a difficult period energy-wise, especially if you woke up on the wrong side of the bed. Don't worry, you can just kick-start your own internal engine—your mind. Your mind is a powerful organ that can enable itself to create energy. All you need to do is to tap this energy reservoir that is already inside of you. And you can achieve this through meditation and mindfulness. This exercise aims to do just that. So get ready to jumpstart your day and get the right amount of energy you need.

The most important thing about this exercise is that you do this very early in the morning… Start when the sun has not yet risen… You will certainly still feel tired and sluggish, but this is part of the experience… You will learn to appreciate more your renewed energy at the end of the exercise if you start early in the day… So get up while the sun has not yet risen…

Pull yourself up from your bed… Do this with great desire even if your bed still calls for you… Resist the temptation to go back to bed… Doing so will kill the intent of this whole exercise… Put some life into your limbs and bones… Rise even if your muscles are not cooperating… Get up… Stand up… Start your day while the sun has not yet started its day….

Try to shake some of the sluggishness off if you can… It's perfectly normal for you to feel like this… After all, you just woke up… And it's so early… But put some energy into your body… It may feel difficult since your energy is in such short supply… But do it anyway…

Straighten your back as you stand… Achieve a good posture… This will surely bring you more energy… And then stretch your arms and legs… Feel the muscles stretch and then relax… Stretch until you can start to feel the muscles warm up…

Bring in desire into each of your movements… You can take your time introducing energy into your body… Do it slowly so that you can ease your way into things… There is no need to do things quickly… The day is still early… You have time for this… You have time to be slow and methodical in bringing your energy levels up…

Start to bring your focus and attention to your breathing… Channel the same desire and intentness you showed earlier to your breath… And feel the added energy that each breath brings…

Breathe in… Hold… And then release…

The tiredness is starting to leave you a little bit… Your head does not feel as heavy as it did when you woke up…

Breathe in… Hold… And then release…

In your wakefulness, you have achieved being in the only place and time that matters... You are in the here and now... And each energetic breath you take brings you to the here and now...

Continue to concentrate on your breathing... Know that your breathing is your key to getting your energy levels up... Your breathing is the key to the ignition... You can fire up your internal engine once you turn the key... Let your breathing enable you to power this engine... So concentrate... Bring in that desire, that intentness...

Breathe in... Hold... And then release...

Breathe in... Hold... And then release...

Breathe in... Hold... And then release...

Prepare yourself, now it's time to turn on the engine... Picture yourself holding the key to the engine... Again, the key is your breathing... You have a firm grasp on it... You are doing it in full concentration... You can feel the desire and intentness with each breath...

Imagine yourself putting the key in the slot... It fits perfectly...

Breathe in... Hold... And then release...

Turn the key... Visualize yourself carefully turning the key... You hear a sound... It's the sound of an engine trying to will itself to life... You put more pressure on the key as you turn it... Picture yourself putting this pressure on the key...

Breathe in... Hold... And then release...

Until you hear a roar! The roar is from your internal engine... You have successfully started it... It roars to life... Its roar is loud... Its roar is proud... It makes an announcement to the whole world... It shouts and screams energy... It starts to pulsate life and vigor... This is your internal engine... And you have kick-started it...

Breathe in... Hold... And then release...

Breathe in... Hold... And then release...

Breathe in... Hold... And then release...

Each breath you take feeds fuel to your internal engine... It is revving more and more... You can feel the power surge... You can feel the energy surge within you... Let this energy continue to grow... Let your engine continue to rev...

You can now feel a sudden rise in temperature... This is the energy that your internal engine produces... Your muscles do not feel listless anymore... On the contrary, they are now full of life... They are ready to move... They are ready for a day full of work... They are ready to let you achieve your goals for the day...

And your head is getting a buzz of great awareness... The energy you are manufacturing from within you is allowing your mind to focus... And it is now focusing on what is important... It is focusing on providing you with more energy... It is focusing on being in the here and now...

Breathe in... Hold... And then release...

Imagine yourself pulsating to the hum of your internal engine... You are revving and vibrating... You are now full of kinetic energy... You are full of anticipation now... You can't wait to get started... You can't wait to move... You have the energy... You have now a good supply of it...

Breathe in... Hold... And then release...

Breathe in... Hold... And then release...

Breathe in... Hold... And then release...

Bring back your focus on your breathing... Your breathing was the key in kick-starting your engine... And it remains the key now for you to feed more fuel to let your engine burn more energy... So continue your focus... Keep your awareness centered on your breathing...

Each breath brings more energy to your being... Let more energy flow into you... Achieve this with each breath that you take in... Do it with great desire...

Your breath and the energy it brings allows you to remain in the here and now... In the here and now you are brimming with energy... In the here and now you are ready to take on the day... In the here and now, you have the capacity to increase your energy levels...

At this point, you should be free from your anxieties... By triggering the ignition of your internal engine, you allowed yourself to get the energy you need... This allowed you to be in the here and now... And in the here and now all your cares and worries do not matter... What matters in the here and now is that you are brimming with life...

Put your cares and worries in the background... Know that thoughts of the past are but memories... They cease to matter in the here and now... And know that thoughts of the future are mere projections... They have not formed any semblance of value yet in the here and now... These things do not matter... The only thing that matters is your energy... It is one with your breathing...

Try to imagine your head now... Imagine it free of the anxieties that haunted you earlier... Your head feels a sense of liberation... It feels light... It can now absorb the energy... Your head is clear... Your mind is ready to take on the challenges the day will bring... It is primed to be at its best...

Breathe in... Hold... And then release...

Each breath not only brings you more energy, but it also puts your anxieties in the background... Be one with your breathing... And just allow the energy to flow... Let the energy power you as you remain in the here and now...

Breathe in... Hold... And then release...

Time to get started... Time to get a move on... You are more than ready to start your day... Your energy level has greatly increased... And it continues to rise... You have successfully kick-started your morning... Try to jump around... Try to jog in place... Shake those energetic arms and legs... Bring more energy to your body...

You can now face the world… Go out of your room… Time to leave your safe place… You are now more than capable of meeting the demands of the day…

DAY 27—GUIDED MEDITATION FOR REDUCING ANXIETY: LISTENING TO THE WIND [30 MINUTES]

Feeling the wind can give you a very relaxing feeling. It also soothes and refreshes you. This exercise will let you experience the goodness of a cool breeze. You can certainly feel the refreshing power of the wind. This exercise will enable you to further practice your mindfulness habit.

This exercise requires you to be outdoors as you need to be able to feel the wind blow. Find a suitable location, preferably a place that you can be alone. It helps if this place is quiet. You want to maximize the experience by being in a place that offers you peace and tranquility. And you can do this any time of the day. But the best time to do this will be early in the morning or during night time after dinner.

Start by going outside and settle into position. Get comfortable and start to let the environment relax you. Sit comfortably but make sure that your back is straight. Or better yet, you can lie down if you can find the opportunity for this. Just make sure that your back is straight the whole time and that your body is not arched in an awkward position. And as you attain relaxation, close your eyes.

Start to feel the air around you… And then bring your attention to your breathing… Be one with your breath… Bring your whole being with you as you breathe… Put in your whole spirit as you execute each inhalation and exhalation… Desire each breath… Want it… Put your whole self in it… Let your spirit flow with your breath…

Breathe in… Hold… And then release…

Let relaxation flow with each breath… Feel the calmness start to overcome your whole body… And let all the tension and tightness escape as you exhale…

Maintain your concentration… Be one with your breath… Be deliberate with each breath… Let each breath be an intentional desire on your part…

Let your breath remind you to be in the here and now… You are in the here and now… And the only thing that matters is you just existing in this time and place… It's just you and your breath… That is your reality… Your reality in the here and now…

Start to feel your surroundings… Can you feel the wind blow? Can you feel the wind's soft touch? Its coolness is slowly caressing your skin… It cools you down, bringing your internal temperature lower… It refreshes you… Feel the relaxation increase as you experience the breeze dancing all around you…

And as you feel the wind, let your breathing flow with it… Let your breathing and the wind flow in unison…

Breathe in… Hold… And then release…

What sensations do you feel as the wind is blowing? What feelings do you derive from the wind touching you? Aside from its cooling effect, what things are brought about by the wind? Let the wind offer you its gifts… Feel them, embrace them… Accept these gifts that the wind brings…

Breathe in… Hold… And then release…

Remember to breathe in unison with the wind's movements… Remember to be in the here and now… This is your reality… You are experiencing the joy of being one with the wind…

Try to rekindle happy memories as the gust of wind blows by you… What do you remember as you feel the refreshing wind pass you by? Try your best to conjure all the delightful memories… These memories are also the wind's gift to you… Take them, accept them… Try to remember… Picture these events in your mind's eye…

Breathe in… Hold… And then release…

Remember to be in the here and now… This is the only place and time that matters…

In the here and now, the wind blows away all the cobwebs that are present in your mind… These cobwebs are your cares and worries… They are your anxieties… Allow the wind to sweep these anxieties away… Let the wind take these apprehensions… There's certainly no need for you to hold on to them… Let these angsts, fears, concerns, and unease disintegrate as they are swept away by the wind… This is another gift that the wind brings you… Accept this gift…

And now you have to listen to what the wind is saying… What is it telling you? What is its message? Go ahead… Try to listen… Train your ears well… Listen carefully… Listen intently… It gives you a soft whisper… It makes the faintest sound, yet this sound reverberates in your mind and heart… Listen to the wind… Listen to what it has to say…

Breathe in… Hold… And then release…

The wind is telling you to let go of the past… The wind is telling you to disregard the future… These things are not in the here and now… They have ceased to matter… Or they do not matter yet… There is no need to let these things invade your thoughts… Listen to the wind… Listen to what it has to say…

And then there is the song that the wind is singing… It is singing a comforting tune… It puts your mind at ease… It sings a song that puts peace in your heart… It sings a song that clears your mind… It is easy on the ears… This song delights your soul… Listen to the song of the wind… And if you can, try to sing along… The tune is familiar to you… You know the words… Go ahead and sing along…

The wind is also giving you advice… Listen to its wisdom… The wind is telling you to go live your life… To just be in the here and now… It assures you that it will be there for you when you need it… The wind will always find a way to sweep your anxieties away… All you need to do is to call for it… All you need to do is to concentrate on your breathing…

Breathe in… Hold… And then release…

Breathe in… Hold… And then release…

Breathe in… Hold… And then release…

You are in the here and now... And in this time and place, you are communing with the wind... You are listening to its whisper... And you are singing a duet with it... It is a song of peace and love... This song takes away all your cares and worries...

Feel the positive effects of your endeavor... The wind has brought you to a very relaxed state... You are in a state of calm... And you feel very refreshed... You are thoroughly enjoying the experience... You are taking full advantage of the wind and its gifts to you...

Go ahead and enjoy the wind... Know that you are in no hurry... So take your time... Commune with the wind... Let your soul continue to communicate with it...

Let your body experience the refreshing feeling of having been recharged by the wind... Feel your energy and power surge as the wind's current around you intensifies... Feel your soul come alive... And let the happy memories flow... Take all of this in and just go with the flow of the wind...

Breathe in... Hold... And then release...

Breathe in... Hold... And then release...

Breathe in... Hold... And then release...

Continue to let your breathing be your focus as you commune with the wind... Take your time... You are in no hurry... Just go with the flow...

You are about to put this meditation exercise to a close... You had a wonderful moment with the wind... Take a few more moments to commune with it... Try to feel its coolness a little bit more... Listen to what it is trying to say one last time... And then thank the wind... Thank the wind for bestowing you its gifts... And make sure to bring these gifts with you as you go...

Breathe in... Hold... And then release...

Breathe in... Hold... And then release...

Breathe in... Hold... And then release...

Maintain the feelings of relaxation and calm... And continue to situate yourself in the here and now...

This exercise has reached its terminus... Get ready to return... As you do, take with you the gifts... And continue to feel relaxed... You will go about your way and return to where you started at the count of three...

Three...

Two...

One...

You may now open your eyes and move your body...

Welcome back!

DAY 28—STRESS-RELIEVING GUIDED MEDITATION—OVERCOMING CHRONIC FATIGUE [30 MINUTES]

Fatigue or extreme tiredness is a normal reaction to stress. As you subject your body to a lot of stress, your body gets tired over time. But to feel this extreme form of tiredness for prolonged periods is not normal anymore. You may be suffering from Chronic Fatigue Syndrome. But know that you can do something about this. You can channel your energy within to properly deal with the stress that you are feeling. In turn, you just might be able to reduce the fatigue and tiredness plaguing you. Try this meditation exercise and reap the benefits of stress relief. You may just discover your fatigue dissipate and your energy levels increased.

Find a comfortable position once again. Go to your identified spot for meditation and make sure this place can give you the peace and quiet you need for this exercise. The best position for your body for this exercise is sitting down. You may sit cross-legged. Just make sure your back is not arched as you do this exercise. Keep your shoulders and neck relaxed. Ease the tensions you feel in these areas of your body. Keep your hands on your lap and let them rest there. Close your eyes and prepare to begin.

You have been feeling very tired lately… In fact, this weariness is starting to affect you… It's bringing you down… It's starting to take a toll on your work… on your life… on your daily existence… You feel this fatigue weighing you down heavily… It is a colossal burden to carry… It adds an additional layer of complication to your already challenging life… And yet the stress continues to pile up… This is because the demands are great… Every single day requires you to be at your best… To put your best foot forward… And you are more than willing to meet and even exceed those demands…

And this causes you a lot of stress… And now you are at the depths of tiredness… You are very fatigued…

Acknowledge this tiredness… Let the weariness out… Feel it… Embrace it… It's part of your existence…

For now, the best thing you can do is to bring your awareness to your breathing…

Breathe in… Hold… And then release…

Feel the momentary relief your breathing gives… Your body needs air… And this air brings goodness inside of you… Let this positivity flow…

Breathe in… Hold… And then release…

Breathe in… Hold… And then release…

Breathe in… Hold… And then release…

Bring in more of it... Let it circulate and let it fill you... Relish the momentary relief it brings... Each breath you take diminishes the stress and the tiredness just a little bit... It makes you feel relaxed... It calms you down...

Let your heartbeat follow the rhythm of your breathing... Then try your best to slow your breathing... So that you may also slow your busy heart... Your heart needs this temporary respite as well... Give it a breather... Breathe in slowly... And do the same as you exhale... Bring in your whole self as you breathe... Be one with it... Breathe with great desire...

Breathe in... Hold... And then release...

Know that your only purpose is to be in the here and now... Acknowledge that you are tired... But bring yourself to the only place and time that matters... Be in the here and now... Achieve this with your breath... Maintain the desire and intentionality with each inhalation and exhalation...

Breathe in... Hold... And then release...

Now try to picture out your whole body... Try to conjure a mental image of your whole being... See in your mind's eye how you look like...

Go ahead and paint that picture in your mind... How do you look? More importantly, how tired do you look?

And as you imagine yourself, try to feel the tiredness that is trying to overcome you right now... How does it feel? Try to put these feelings into words... This is how you acknowledge your tiredness... This is how you tell your fatigue and stress that you know that they exist... This is the first step in trying to ease them away from you... You have to first notice that they are there... Be aware of the exhaustion that you are feeling...

Breathe in... Hold... And then release...

Know that in the here and now you are tired... And this is perfectly acceptable... The human body has its limits... And you have reached yours... Acknowledge this... This is your reality...

Try now to feel which areas of your body are particularly tired... Trace your whole being from head to foot... Start with the soles of your feet... Feel the tiredness there... And then move your way up... Move up until you reach your head... And then feel the fatigue in each of these areas...

Breathe in... Hold... And then release...

Now start to take an inventory of these areas that are particularly tired... These are the areas that have reached their limit... You might have subjected so much stress to these areas because of all the worldly demands that you have to fulfill...

Feel proud of these body parts... These are the parts that worked so hard to keep you standing... These are the body parts that allowed you to taste success... These are the parts that enabled you to be the best that you can be... So give these parts the credit that is due them... Commend them... Worship their feats of greatness... Be proud of your fatigue... It enabled you to do great things...

And now it's time to let the tiredness pass... Your body needs to rest and recover... So it's time to relieve your body of its stress... Again, be one with your breathing... Let your breathing bring you relaxation... Let your breathing sweep the stress away...

Breathe in... Hold... And then release...

Imagine that the air surrounding you as a form of energy... This energy, once taken in by the body, offers relief... It dissolves the stress away... It disintegrates the fatigue that you feel...

Breathe in... Hold... And then release...

Bring in all the energy from your environment... And then feel them work inside of you... These energies are cleansing you... They target the stress and fatigue in your body and they start to work on them... Little by little, slowly but surely, the stress and fatigue are being broken down by the energy that you breathe... So take more of it...

Breathe in... Hold... And then release...

Breathe in... Hold... And then release...

Breathe in... Hold... And then release...

Holding your breath allows this energy to flow faster inside of you... As they flow, they blow past all the stress that is precariously hanging on to your body parts... This energy sweeps them away... This energy is collecting the stress and tiredness because it will try to bring them out of you...

Breathe in... Hold... And then release...

And as you exhale, you can feel the stress and tiredness leave your body... The stress and tiredness are being carried off by your exhalation... You can feel relief from the malaise with each breath you blow out... You actually feel better now... You are starting to feel more relaxed...

Continue with the rhythm of your breathing... Breathe slowly... Do it at a pace that is unhurried... There is no need to rush... Know that relieving your body of stress takes time... Know that the process of diminishing your fatigue is a slow and methodical endeavor...

Breathe in... Hold... And then release...

Let each breath continue to bring you the good energy from your surroundings... Hold your breath and feel the energy work inside you... Feel it wipe away the stress and fatigue you feel... And then feel the delight of stress-relief after every exhalation... Allow yourself to feel more relaxed... Let calmness overcome you now... Feel your body become unburdened... It is now unshackled from the fatigue that held it down earlier... Feel the liberation... You have freedom from stress now... Relish it... Enjoy it...

Breathe in... Hold... And then release...

Breathe in... Hold... And then release...

Breathe in... Hold... And then release...

Remember to be in the only place and time that matters... You are in the here and now... And in the here and now you are being relieved of the pressure of stress... Your body is now recovering... It is resting well... It is preparing itself to do more, to achieve more...

Continue to put your thoughts and effort in your breathing... Be one with it... Bring your whole awareness to it... Your breathing is the key to achieving stress relief...

Breathe in... Hold... And then release...

And now it's time for you to return to your day... You have greatly decreased your stress levels... You are now liberated from the fatigue that bothered you... Feel the lightness of your being... You can now go back to your day with more energy...

Try to bring life back to your muscles... Move them, slowly at first... You can change your sitting position, but continue to keep your back straight... And when you are ready, open your eyes...

DAY 29—STARING AT THE MONSTER & FACING THE ANXIETIES WITHIN: GUIDED MEDITATION TO OVERCOME ANXIETY [30 MINUTES]

Close your eyes and prepare yourself… You are going on an adventure…

Are you ready? It's fine if you're not… Take your time to prepare…

It seems that you are hesitating… Don't you want to go and have this adventure? What's the adventure about, you ask? Well, you are going on a quest to quash a monster… This monster's name is Anxiety…

Oh, so that's why you hesitate… You can feel this monster within you… Do you have this monster inside of you right now? Do you have anxieties?

Ah, so it seems you have anxieties within you… This is perfectly normal… Everyone has them… That's why you are going on an adventure… Your trepidation is perfectly understandable… After all, you don't have the slightest idea of how to deal with this monster… Is this the thing that bothers you?

If it is, then worry not… I have a gift for you… It will help you in conquering your anxieties…

Here, accept my gift… This is your weapon… It is the sword of mindfulness… It's no ordinary sword… It has a special power… The power of this sword is that it can vanquish the monster within… And in order to put power in the sword, you have to be one with your breathing… Listen and follow what I say… Listen well…

Breathe in… Hold… And then release…

Do you see your sword glowing? That's because you powered it with your breath… Awareness of your breathing brings you in the here and now… The here and now is the only place and time that matters… Your weapon is at its most efficient if you bring yourself to the here and now… Let's continue to power up your sword…

Breathe in… Hold… And then release…

Breathe in… Hold… And then release…

Breathe in… Hold… And then release…

Have you noticed anything else happening to you? Do you feel more relaxed now? Try and take notice of the sensations trying to course through your body… You can actually feel your whole body getting lighter… The tension and tightness of your muscles have disappeared… This is the effect of being one with your breath… And this relaxation that you are feeling now is your armor… It is another one of my gifts to you… This armor of relaxation will protect you from the monster you will be facing off with…

Bring more power to your weapon and to your armor… Incorporate your whole desire to your breath… Concentrate and give it life… Your awareness on your breath matters… Be deliberate… Be intentional… Breathe so that you can obtain great power… Breathe so that you can be in the here and now… This is what you will be needing as you face off with the monster…

Breathe in… Hold… And then release…

Breathe in… Hold… And then release…

Breathe in… Hold… And then release…

It is time to set foot on our journey… It's time to embark on our adventure… Get ready to meet the monster… And then do your best to vanquish it…

A little bit further and you shall reach your destination… You can now see the outline of the monster… You can see anxiety… You can see your anxieties… You didn't have to travel far and wide to find your anxieties… It's because your anxieties just reside within you…

Slowly approach the beast… Announce your arrival… Tell the beast what you intend to do with it… Tell the monster that you will vanquish it… You will make it submit… You will defeat it…

Don't be intimidated by it… It may shout and roar… It may gesture violently at you… But trust me when I tell you that it cannot hurt you… It cannot hurt you if you will not allow it to… Your anxieties need your permission and consent… If you don't give it, then it cannot do anything to you… It cannot harm you…

But you are starting to feel fear… You are fearing the unknown… You are starting to get scared of what is to come… You are thinking up adverse scenarios in your mind… This is what this monster does to you… It makes you overthink… It makes you overanalyze… It loves to bring you to a place and time that has yet to be… It likes to strip you of your confidence as it offers you glimpses of an uncertain future…

Don't allow your anxieties to do this to you… Again, it needs your consent… Banish the thought away from your mind…

Be in the here and now… Remember your weapon and your armor… Use them…

Breathe in… Hold… And then release…

Breathe in… Hold… And then release…

Breathe in… Hold… And then release…

Slay those thoughts of uncertainty… Slay those thoughts of a frightful future… They have yet to happen… They do not matter…

Breathe in… Hold… And then release…

You thrust a swift blow to the monster in front of you… It shouts in pain… It retreats… It is down, but not out… And now it starts to retaliate…

Now you are starting to feel dread again… But this time it's a different feeling that this monster is trying to throw at you… This time, the monster is making you feel regret… Regret of the past… This is your past where mistakes were made… And now you are starting to feel guilt… You look to the past with shame and embarrassment… If only you could undo things… If only you could have set things right back then…

You start to feel the heaviness of the past… This weight is pulling you down… You feel the gravity of your body being doubled… You can hardly stand… You want to fall down… You want to give in to the monster…

But do not give in… Do not give consent to it… You do not need to feel this way… Do not allow it to let you feel these emotions…

The past is done… You can no longer do anything about the past… Probably the only thing you can do is to accept them… Accept the hurt and the pain… Accept the sorrow that it brings… Accept the regret and the guilt… You cannot go back to the past and undo the hurt and the pain… But you can do something about it in the here and now…

And this is where you stand… You are in the here and now… And right here, right now, you are facing the monster… You are facing your anxieties… And you have your weapon to vanquish it… Fight the monster…

You lift your sword with both your hands, not giving in to the power of your anxieties… You raise your sword and point it at the monster… And the monster now knows that it is powerless… You have managed to overcome its tricks… You successfully brushed away the thoughts of uncertainty… You have successfully moved on from the pain of the past… Now let the blade of mindfulness pierce through the monster… It's time to crush anxiety…

Breathe in… Hold… And then release…

And down goes anxiety with one swift blow… It lies on the ground, clutching the wound that your mindfulness sword delivered… It is holding on for dear life…

You look at the eyes of the monster and you see something very familiar… The eyes you are gazing at are the same eyes as the ones on your face… They are your eyes too… You and your anxiety share the same eyes… You look at both the future and past the same… This is the truth about your anxieties… And this truth is what will liberate you… For if you share the same eyes with this monster, you can have control over what it sees…

Control… That is what you need… And know that you have it… If you do not give consent, if you do not give control to your anxieties, then it can never harm you… And you have the power to vanquish it… You just have to tap this power that is already within you…

You look at the creature that you defeated… It is no longer the scary creature that once intimidated you… In its vanquished state, you can see it for what it really is… You can see that it is surmountable… It's just a challenge you need to go through…

Just realize that all it takes for you to defeat your anxieties is the weapon of mindfulness... It's just a matter of being in the here and now... Right here, right now, your past ceases to matter... They are all but done with... Right here, right now, the future has yet to come... They also do not matter... What matters is that you exist in the present... And you have all the means to take control of your life... This is what you just did... And this is what you shall continue to do...

Breathe in... Hold... And then release...

Breathe in... Hold... And then release...

Breathe in... Hold... And then release...

Celebrate your victory... Marvel at the fact that you were able to strike down the monster that was within you... Be proud that you were able to stare through the eyes of the monster... Doing so meant that you were brave enough to do it...

Breathe in... Hold... And then release...

Continue to remain in the here and now... Continue to bring awareness to your breathing...

You are victorious... This means that the adventure is over... Congratulations on your victory... You may now return, if you wish... You shall return after the count of three...

Three...

Two...

One...

DAY 30—GUIDED SLEEP MEDITATION: OFF TO LA-LA LAND... [40 MINUTES]

Welcome to the last exercise in this book. It has been quite a ride. And to give your experience a delightful close, your last exercise will deliver you in a very restive state. This exercise will guide you so that you can be off to a place of deep slumber. Prepare yourself and in a few moments, you should be off dreaming...

Prepare your bedroom like the previous sleep exercise. Make sure that noise and other obtrusive sounds are at the minimum. Also, look into the temperature of the room—not too cold and not too hot. And then turn off the lights. Or you may just turn them down. Dim lights will also suffice for this exercise.

Lie down on your bed and get inside the covers. Attain a very comfortable position and get ready for a good night's rest. But take note that this is not just any other night of sleep. Tonight, you will be whisked away off to a far-away place.... This place is where magic exists and your fantasies become reality... You will be journeying the dream world...

Start by removing any distractions away from you... Try to eliminate thoughts that are currently haunting your mind... These things are not needed where you're going... You can perhaps remove distractions better by getting in touch with your breathing... Be mindful of your breathing... Follow its rhythm... And try to bring desire with each breath you take...

Breathe in... Hold... And then release...

Breathe in... Hold... And then release...

Breathe in... Hold... And then release...

Feel relaxation start to invade your body... Allow this relaxation to make your body feel very light... As if it's floating on air... And in fact, you are now floating... You are flying off to the sky... You are riding a cloud... It is soft and warm and fluffy... And this cloud whisks you away from your bedroom... And now you can find yourself flying off into the darkness of the night sky... You can see your house below you... A little bit higher the cloud goes and you can now see the whole town...

Let the cloud take you to a magical place... Let the cloud bring you to the world of the dreaming... Just lie down and relax... There is no need to worry... The cloud will keep you safe... It will never let you fall... You feel safe riding your cloud...

Breathe in... Hold... And then release...

And now the cloud you are riding transforms itself into a white steed... You are now riding such a majestic animal as it gallops its way to the clouds... And it slowly stops to where a rainbow is perched... Your white horse stops to let you appreciate the colors of the rainbow...

You can see the warm reds and oranges... These colors bring energy inside of you... And then you can see the calming yellows and greens... These colors bring a certain peace into your being... And of course, you can see the cool violets and blues... They give you a sense of security... The sight of these colors brings you great joy... You marvel at them and you take them all in... You try to let the rainbow penetrate your soul... It boosts your spirit...

Breathe in... Hold... And then release...

Breathe in... Hold... And then release...

Breathe in... Hold... And then release...

Your steed is slowly approaching a castle... The gates of the castle open and your white horse safely lands... You dismount your steed and slowly make your way inside... And then you realize that the castle is yours... You are the monarch that rules over this kingdom that you find yourself in... You are the ruler of your dream world...

You go inside the castle and sit on your throne... And there's a show before you... You can see in front of you all the happy memories you had... It is played before you like a movie... And this gives you great delight... You are enjoying the memories that are played out before you... All this as you sit on your throne... You start to reminisce... You start to feel a sense of longing...

You get up from your throne and start to wander off from your castle... You make your way to the inner recesses of your castle... And soon you find yourself in the treasure room... This is the room where your greatest treasure is kept... You open the treasure chest and you gaze at the treasure... This is your treasure... This is what you hold dear the most... It is there in front of you... It is safely hidden in the treasure room of your castle...

Go ahead and look at it... What does it look like? See the silhouette of your treasure... And also see all the contours, the lines, the curves, the swirls... See everything about it... What do you see? What is this treasure that you keep inside a secure treasure chest? This is something that is most important to you... And it is only you who can see it... It is only you who can appreciate its greatest value...

Breathe in... Hold... And then release...

Breathe in... Hold... And then release...

Breathe in... Hold... And then release...

It's time to close the treasure chest... You need to go out of your castle... You are yearning for an adventure... So go out and venture the far places... These are places contained in your dreaming world waiting to be discovered... And you actually have the opportunity to go to these magnificent places...

Take your white steed with you... Ride the majestic beast and feel it bring you swiftly to your destination... It takes you to a wonderful place... It is full of magical creatures... Take a few moments to take everything in... Try to see this place... Try to observe the fine details... Try to see with your mind's eye all the magnificent creatures that are present...

Gathered with you are a few people... You look around and see familiar faces... The faces you see are those of people who are close to you... These are the people that are dear to you... These are the people you care about and love...

They have gathered to let you know that they want to go with you on your journey... These people who are dear to you also yearn for the same kind of adventure that now fills your heart... And you are glad to hear this from them...

And so you and your party start preparing... You have determined that there is much more of the dreaming world to explore... You want to experience and witness the magic and splendor of the place... You and your group are heading off to la-la land...

Your adventure has started... You have instructed your group to get going... You are filled with excitement... There's a certain rush that starts to fill you... This is the joy you are getting as you dream... This is what the dreaming world gives you... Enjoy the moment... You can look forward to the great adventure that is up ahead... And you have the people that you love and care about going with you...

Your heart is filled with great contentment... You feel warm inside... You find yourself in a place that is safe... You find yourself in a place that fulfills each of your fantasies... This is the dreaming world that you find yourself in...

Feel free to continue your exploration of the dreaming world... Go ahead and take that adventure... Try to experience what the dreaming world has to offer you... Know that you own this place... Know that you are safe and secure in your own dreaming world...

And now you can start to allow the relaxation of sleep to bring you farther into the dreaming world... You are feeling so still... You are feeling so calm... You have totally let go of the waking world... In fact, nothing from the waking world exists where you are right now... Know that you are in a magical place full of wonder and excitement... And this place is yours for the taking... So go ahead and explore some more... This is your dreaming world...

You are starting to feel more and more relaxed... Everything is becoming feathery light... The waking world has finally released you from its clutches... It can no longer hold you down... You are free to be wherever you wish to be... You are free to roam and explore your dreaming world...

Breathe in... Hold... And then release...

Breathe in... Hold... And then release...

Breathe in... Hold... And then release...

Everything is quiet... everything is still... All you can hear is your heartbeat... And the faint sound of your breathing... Everything starts to fade... It starts to fade to black... Until all you see is nothing... Embrace the nothingness... Let it bring you peace...

Sleep... Sleep well... Sweet dreams... See you in the dreaming world...

www.ingramcontent.com/pod-product-compliance
Lightning Source LLC
Chambersburg PA
CBHW081414080526
44589CB00016B/2527